HIGHER SELF *Habits*

The Scientific, Strategic, and Spiritual Framework to Get Out of Your Own Way — *For Good*

ALESSIA CITRO

FOREWORD BY DR. JENNIFER CHRISMAN

Published by inhabit LLC
alessiacitro.com

Disclaimer: This publication is designed to provide accurate and authoritative information regarding the subject matter covered.

The author of this book does not dispense medical or professional advice or prescribe the use of any technique as a form of treatment for physical, emotional, or medical problems without the advice of a professional, either directly or indirectly. The intent of the author is only to offer information of a general nature to help you in your quest for personal growth and well-being. In the event you use any of the information in this book for yourself, the author and the publisher assume no responsibility for your actions.

The advice and strategies contained herein may not be suitable for your situation. You should consult with a professional where appropriate. Neither the author nor the publisher guarantees any specific level of success and accepts no responsibility for any losses or damages incurred. By reading this book, you accept that you are responsible for your own actions and decisions. This book is intended to educate, entertain, and inspire the reader.

Book Cover Design by ebooklaunch.com, Ginger Hamilton of Ginger CC Design LLC, and Alessia Citro
Interior Design by Sophie Hanks
Illustrations by Alessia Citro

ISBN: 979-8-9906552-1-8

First Edition 2024

For more information, visit alessiacitro.com
Follow on Instagram at @alessiacitro__

Dedication

For Jeff, my husband, partner, best friend, and unicorn. Thank you for always supporting me and loving me in every way, and through my many versions and evolutions.

For Mila, my darling girl. Thank you for being my *why*, for shining such a bright light in the world, and for being the most beautiful and playful teacher that I never knew I needed in this game of life.

For Mom and Dad. Thank you for being the sturdy net and loving arms that have always allowed me to leap and fall.

For Luverne and Anne Marie, my beloved grandparents. Thank you for setting the bar for the art of living, and for continuing to guide me and inspire me from the other side. I love and miss you both.

For the visionaries who seek their calling courageously. (That's *you!*)

"We ask ourselves, 'Who am I to be brilliant, gorgeous, talented, and fabulous?' Actually, who are you not to be?"

—Marianne Williamson, *A Return to Love*

Table of Contents

Foreword 7

Start Here: Your Upward Spiral Begins 11

Part One: Aware...**23**

Chapter 1: The Power of Intention 25

Chapter 2: The Slow and Steady Strategy 33

Chapter 3: All-or-Nothing Is Your Achilles Heel...............39

Chapter 4: Keep It Simple 49

Chapter 5: Overcoming Limiting Beliefs and Self-Judgment.........63

Chapter 6: Reframing Your Internal and External Experience 81

Chapter 7: Common Fears and How to Move Past Them...............91

Part Two: Align...**107**

Chapter 8: Expand Your Perception to Expand Your Legacy.......109

Chapter 9: Be Her Now: The Power of the Quantum 125

Chapter 10: Higher Self Identity.......................................135

Chapter 11: Higher Self Energetics 151

Part Three: Audit..**161**

Chapter 12: Put Out the Fire to Clear the Smoke 163

Chapter 13: Thought, Word, and Deed 181

Chapter 14: Outward Embodiment 193

Chapter 15: Inputs Determine Outputs 199

Part Four: Activate **213**

Chapter 16 : Domino Habits...215

Chapter 17: Build on Steel with Behavioral Science Basics............221

Chapter 18: Crafting Habits to Create Your Dream Life.................249

Chapter 19: Bless and Release Negative Habits..............................267

Part Five: Ascend and Amplify **281**

Chapter 20: You Are Revolutionary 283

A Plea to Your Higher Self...289

Appendix: Addiction Resources 291

Acknowledgments 293

Endnotes...299

Foreword

Inside the self-improvement and personal development space, there is no shortage of books promising transformation and offering strategies for achieving one's highest potential. Yet, every once in a while, there is a rare gem that stands out—a book born from the trenches by someone who has walked the path themselves, who has confronted the edges of their own growing pains, and who has emerged as a beacon of inspiration for others.

Higher Self Habits is that book. Written by a woman who embodies the very principles she shares.

I had the privilege of meeting Alessia Citro during a time of massive transition in her life, when she was grappling with the complexities of her own journey, moving away from a corporate career and toward entrepreneurship, and from disconnection to self-realization. I witnessed firsthand her unwavering commitment to understanding the intricacies of human behavior, the depths of her own psyche, and the transformative power of habitual practices. Her journey was not one of mere intellectual curiosity; it was a deeply personal quest for meaning, purpose, and fulfillment.

What sets Alessia apart is not just her expertise or her mastery of self-help principles—it is her authenticity. She isn't just spouting theories or regurgitating the same tried approaches; she is a living testament to the power of the practices she teaches. She is the embodiment of walking the talk. In her, you will find not just a guide but a fellow traveler, someone who has already navigated the terrain of the mind and soul with courage, resilience, and grace.

I was in the room the day she openly shared that she thought she might have a problem with drinking too much and embarked on the journey of what would eventually become sobriety and helping other women break free from the habit of escaping through alcohol.

I watched as she stepped away from and shut down the business she had left her corporate job to launch because she was willing to acknowledge that it was out of alignment and built on the egoic desire for accomplishment, profit, and recognition. Her willingness to pull all the way back, to shut it all down, and to really go inward so that she could *know* her mission, is the reason you are holding this book now.

Alessia's courage to go first and be the living example of Higher Self Habits is how you now have a blueprint for aligning and designing your own Higher Self Habits.

This concept may sound lofty, perhaps even esoteric, but at its core lies a simple truth: our daily habits shape our destiny. Habits are the invisible architecture of daily life. We repeat approximately 40 percent of our behavior almost daily, which means our habits shape our existence, as well as our future. If we change our habits, we can change our entire lives. The question we need to ask and that this book will help answer is: how often do we approach our habits with intention, with mindfulness, and with the awareness that they are the building blocks of our Higher Self?

Alessia invites us to embark on a journey of self-discovery, to peel back the layers of conditioning and societal expectations, and to reclaim our agency in shaping our destinies. Drawing from a variety of psychological insights, spiritual wisdom, and personal anecdotes, she guides us through a process of self-inquiry and self-transformation. Each chapter is not just a collection of theories but a roadmap for cultivating habits that nourish the soul, empower the spirit, and awaken us to our highest potential.

But perhaps what is most compelling about Alessia's work is her humility. She does not claim to have all the answers, nor does she profess to have attained some lofty state of enlightenment. Instead, she invites us to join her on a journey of continual growth and evolution, reminding us that the path to our Higher Self is not a destination but a lifelong pilgrimage.

As you embark on this journey through the pages of this book, may you be inspired by Alessia's courage, authenticity, and unwavering commitment to embodying her highest and best self. May you discover within yourself the power to transcend limitations, to cultivate habits that nourish your soul, and to live a life of purpose, passion, and fulfillment. And may you, like Alessia, become a beacon of light, illuminating the path for others to follow.

—Dr. Jennifer Chrisman

Start Here
Your Upward Spiral Begins

*"Do not despise the bottom rungs in the ascent
to greatness."*

—Publilius Syrus

Freedom is the promise of *Higher Self Habits* and my number
one value. Perhaps you picked this book up because you value it
too and want more of it. I got you, my friend.

First, let's address the elephant in the room. Habits sound
constricting and boring AF. (Is it okay if I use colorful language?
Hope so, because it's scattered throughout these pages.)
Hearing the word "habit" made me think of a corset ... around
my life. It's why I largely avoided habits for my first thirty-six
years in favor of spontaneity and the pursuit of, you guessed it:
freedom.

The irony is that habits are *the* path to the spaciousness
and freedom we seek. They are *the* vehicle to next-level us.
And habits get to be fun! I'll prove it. While I do, if you actively
integrate what you learn in this book, you will have changed by
the time you reach the back cover. And, you'll have a good time
doing it. You can take that to the bank.

Speaking of change, we humans tend to avoid it. We say we want transformation, but the survival mechanisms of our brain and ego do everything possible to make us stay the same. Kathy Overman states this perfectly: "Your nervous system will always choose a familiar hell over an unfamiliar heaven." Luckily, we can override this wiring and ascend into a higher version of ourselves with the right method and blueprint. You're holding that blueprint—the *Higher Self Habits* method—in your hands right now.

Here's the other truth about change. Most of us will change only when we've hit rock bottom, get an ultimatum, or when we feel like we're circling the drain. If you're not in a position like this, standing to lose something precious, *good*. I'd like to help you avoid these scenarios. And if you are there … well, I was too. I lived to tell about it, and so will you. The customizable framework in these pages will help you climb the mountain step-by-step in a manageable way.

So, yes, change can be hard, but it's possible. I'm walking proof it can be done—and in a relatively short period of time. Here are a few of the ways I've changed in the last few years:

- I went from grinding in corporate tech sales at Houzz, Salesforce, and Google to walking away and becoming an entrepreneur.
- Initially, I carried toxic traits and burnout from my corporate life into entrepreneurship. I had to make massive course corrections for my health, finances, and family. Now, I'm soul-centered, balanced, and in aligned flow. (Most of the time. I'm a work in progress who needs this book too.)

- Until I had my daughter, I often said unkind things about people. Becoming a mom forced a needed perspective shift. Now, I'm vigilant about avoiding gossip and withholding judgment.

- When I spoke badly of others or judged them, I did the same to myself. I've largely shifted from self-loathing to self-love. It hasn't been easy, but it's been worth it.

- For most of my life, I loved provoking debates and winning them (or thinking I did). I especially enjoyed riling people up about politics. Thank God I knocked that off! Today I'm focused on keeping my peace and doing what I can to remind others that we have more in common than we do not.

- From 2019–2022, I was very successful selling wine online. In two years, I built a seven-figure business and a team of nearly 1,000 people (mostly women and mothers) to sell wine alongside me. But there was a dark side to the success. The COVID-19 pandemic created the perfect storm for my alcohol use disorder to escalate and to profit off others struggling with it too. In January 2022, I finally awakened to this misalignment and walked away from the business. Then in June 2022, I quit drinking and, ultimately, quit for good on April 1, 2023. Since then, I have helped dozens of others get sober—many of whom are women who had been in the business with me.

- For my first thirty-six years, I was largely focused on doing, achieving, chasing accolades, and finding success. I wore busy like a badge of honor. I'm now focused on who I'm *being*. Fulfillment and impact on others are now my drivers—particularly helping others craft their dream lives through habits and awakening them to their potential and hidden genius.

- I went from needing to control everything to detaching from outcomes and letting the universe take the steering wheel ... as much as possible. I finally realized it has far better plans than I do!

Maybe you don't have such glaring problems or "flaws." Perhaps you just want to change your outlook to feel happier and more whole. What's contained in this book can help there too.

As a matter of fact, I saw the glass as half empty from a young age. One of my childhood friends didn't invite me to her birthday party when we were nine. I was gutted and asked why. Thank God I did because the answer changed my life. The reason I was not invited was because her mom believed I was a negative influence ... and I *was* negative! I had taken on the complaining and negativity from some of my family members as my own. Can you relate to being influenced by those around you, for better or worse? That conversation became a line in the sand of my life. I began to shed the negative perspective and complaining I'd acquired. Now, I can reframe to find a silver lining in anything. Are *you* ready to begin seeing everything from a perspective of advantage and opportunity? You won't be able to help it by the time you hit the back cover.

Reflecting on how we've acted in the past can be painful, but noting our growth and progress is a powerful lever in continuing to change and grow. It's why this book exists. I was scared shitless to start my *Higher Self Habits* coaching programs and write this book. My impostor syndrome was enormous. I thought of all the mistakes I've made and the many reasons why anyone besides me should write this book. But *those are the very reasons I am exactly the person to write it.* Seeing how far I've come helped me see how far I can go. And the same is true for you!

Now that we've reviewed my shortcomings shortlist, let's get back to the subject of this book: *you.* This book is for and about you and the people you're going to impact by becoming your Higher Self ... should you answer the call. Perhaps you've been sending that call to voicemail for various reasons. Sometimes, it's not a good time to level up. *Call me back in a year, Higher Self!*

Maybe you see the distance between where you are and where you want to be, and that chasm terrifies you into staying put. Or it could be you don't feel you're "enough" yet. You aren't ready enough, worthy enough, good enough, qualified enough, thin enough, etc. If you're in either camp, know this book will offer you a sturdy bridge you can walk across one step at a time.

Other times, we worry about what others will think of us if we pursue our dreams. Particularly if you, too, have a shortcomings shortlist. (We'll cover this further in Chapters 6 and 8.)

Whatever the reasons you haven't embraced becoming your favorite version of you, to all this, I say ... fuck it. Seriously. Yes, the gap between your desired future and where you are now might be vast. But you've grown significantly already. No doubt or you surely wouldn't be reading a book in this genre.

A powerful antidote to these worries and feelings of fear is gratitude. It is an undercurrent that runs through this book. Can you begin to feel grateful for every setback or problem, just like you would for a blessing? Can you begin to see each obstacle as a steppingstone and strength-training exercise for the abundance that awaits you? As you read these pages and reflect on the applications to your life, I invite you to keep gratitude at the forefront of your mind. It will begin to change everything.

Here's another reason stepping into your Higher Self matters: the divine law of unity. It states that everything in the universe is interconnected, and all beings are part of a unified whole. Because we are all one, when you take strides in becoming the person you were created to be, you will initiate a far-reaching, vast ripple effect of goodness. You'll make waves! You may never know the extent of your impact, but the world will be better for you having lived.

One of my favorite movies of all time is *Gladiator*. In it, a young and strapping Russell Crowe plays Maximus, a general in Marcus Aurelius' Roman army who is forced into slavery. As Maximus says in an opening scene, "What we do in life echoes in eternity." What will *your* echo be?

Before we go further, let's level-set about religion and spirituality. Whether you are devout to a particular religion, "church hurt," an atheist, "woo-woo," New Age, or somewhere in between, so long as you are striving to be a better version of yourself, I wrote this book for you. Obviously, this book has a spiritual bent (the title and subtitle should've given that away), but please know this book is meant to meet you wherever you are on your spiritual journey and in your beliefs.

You'll sometimes see me use terms including God, the creator, the universe, Higher Power, Spirit, and Source. I use these interchangeably. You have full permission to substitute terms so they work for you. Take what serves you; leave what doesn't.

When I refer to the Higher Self, I imagine the divine in each of us. Given the book's title, defining this term provides helpful context.

The Higher Self represents the highest, most evolved, and spiritually aware aspect of an individual's consciousness, often seen as the part of a person connected to a higher or divine source of wisdom, love, and guidance. The Higher Self possesses a deep understanding of one's life purpose, spiritual path, and the interconnectedness of all things.

The Higher Self is:

- In tune with spiritual truths and transcendent of the ego
- Unconditionally loving and compassionate
- Intuitive, with a deep inner knowing and sense of purpose
- Aligned and intent on fulfilling the soul's journey
- Connected to the divine, universal consciousness, and infinite intelligence

I believe the Higher Self resides in each of us, waiting to be called upon and brought into the world through our authentic, individual expression.

With that, let's also be clear about who the Higher Self *is not* and potential perversions that our ego might attempt to sneak past us. This pursuit of ascending into a better version of ourselves does not mean being perfect, holier-than-thou, self-righteous, and hard-driving. We are going to continue making mistakes and fucking up as we level up. In case you verge on all-or-nothing thinking (more on that soon) and you had been visualizing your Higher Self in a halo, donning a white robe as angelic arias play in the distance, that f-bomb was for you, to lovingly snap you out of your trance. Yes, we absolutely have the divine in us. And yet, we're human. We need to be realistic about what this process of *becoming* looks like. Stepping into your Higher Self might mean you start farting angel dust ... but I wouldn't count on it.

Since a secret to a happy life is properly managing expectations, let's wrap up this chapter with what you'll find in the rest of the book.

Without exaggeration, I've read hundreds of books across self-help, spirituality, neuroscience, behavioral science, and the quantum. Attended countless conferences and retreats. Invested in coaches and various forms of therapy. Became a certified life coach myself. Listened to thousands of hours of personal development podcasts. I've done all the things. And what I found was a dichotomy. These resources tend to focus on science, strategy, *or* spirituality. Rarely did I find one that spanned more than one of these genres. For a holistic approach, we need flexible strategy backed by science and a spiritual connection.

When science, spirit, and strategy are separate and siloed, it creates a gap and ignores half of our nature. After all, *we are spiritual beings having a physical experience.* This book holds that belief at the forefront. To feel whole, we must balance both masculine and feminine energies. These energies have nothing to do with gender. They are the polarity of complementary opposites: the yin and the yang, the black and the white, the north and the south. In these pages, I strive to marry the feminine energies of *being*—spirituality, soul, feeling, and flow—with the structure and masculine energies of *doing*—strategy, habits, analysis, and behavior change. To thrive, we need both sides of this energetic coin in balance. So yes, you will find some "woo-woo" in this book, but I back it all up with scientific principles and data. And when facts boost your belief, your personal results get a boost too.

If you've read other books on habits and haven't had lasting results, the above might be why. Make no mistake—the habits books I've read have helped me change my life. I will quote and reference some of their insights and strategies in this book. And then I'll pair them with why they matter *on a soul level*.

I noticed something else about the habits books available. Nearly every single one is written by a man. With few exceptions, this genre is absolutely dominated by male authors. Habits shape our lives, and I thought it was time to bring a woman's perspective to this important subject. Like anything, the wider the available viewpoints, the clearer the picture and the better off we all are for it. This will be unlike any other habits book you've picked up in that it focuses heavily on the *why* and the *who* (that's you) before showing you the *what*, *when*, and *how*. My goal is to stand apart from every other habits book available today by providing a holistic approach that offers lasting transformation. (Shameless ask here: If you get value from this book, please tell your friends!)

There are five stages to the *Higher Self Habits* method outlined in this book. Blending science with spirit, this is a flexible framework you can customize to your individual needs that meets you where you are. Below is a brief synopsis of the method and corresponding parts of this book. (If you like a short overview before you dig into a book, this next section is for you. If you don't, skip to the end of the short list below and get started.)

Part One: *Aware.* We cannot address or begin solving a problem until we are aware it exists. In this stage, we address many reasons we inadvertently hold ourselves back or stumble through self-betterment. If you are anything like my coaching clients and me, this part will likely feel validating, empowering, and invigorating.

Part Two: *Align.* We begin coming into remembrance of our true nature and get clear on who we are and who we authentically want to be. Get ready to go deep. Ideators and dreamers will especially enjoy this stage.

Part Three: *Audit.* This stage is more fun than it sounds, and it's my favorite in the process. Here, you'll take an honest inventory of what to stop, start, and continue, and you'll be given a framework to inform exactly where to begin making changes.

Part Four: *Activate.* This is where the rubber meets the road and we put it all together. I'll teach you how to design your way in and out of any behavior and how to bring about lasting change. Perhaps one of the best takeaways from this stage is that it's so simple, you can use it repeatedly and teach it to your partner, kids, roommate, etc.

Part Five: *Ascend and Amplify.* This is the culmination of the first revolution in your upward spiral. Once you've gone through the four stages of the method, you'll look back on your starting point and be blown away by your progress. You'll have elevated (ascended) into a better version of yourself, experiencing expanded capacity and confidence. When you're out in the world, you'll radiate (amplify) a higher frequency that will make others take note. You'll become aware of new levels of growth, and the process begins again. Thus, an upward spiral.

Perhaps this is ingrained in me from my tech sales days, but I prefer to undersell and overdeliver. As such, I don't want to puff you up too much about the results you'll experience from reading and applying this book, but here's what I know is true. Whether it's gaining self-confidence by keeping promises to yourself, becoming organized, being more intentional, or showing up in the world as an upgraded version of yourself—this book will catapult you on your journey to becoming your Higher Self. I know because I did it, and my clients are doing it too. Now it's your turn.

This book is meant to be an immersive experience. In each chapter, you'll find simple exercises and reflections that invite you to *be her now*, as in, *be your Higher Self now*. Taking a few minutes or less to do these will supercharge your results. You can use a journal or download and print the companion workbook available at alessiacitro.com/book. There's a Spotify playlist for you at that link too!

You have other free resources available, which I'll note throughout. These can be found at alessiacitro.com/book.

If you need additional support at any point, check out alessiacitro.com/programs or shoot me a message through Instagram or the contact form on my website. You got this, and I'm with you every step of the way!

BE HER NOW REFLECTION AND EXERCISE:

- Create your own shortcomings shortlist. Are you viewing these as disqualifications? Or as qualifications? What are all the ways you've changed, elevated, and evolved?
- Have you been holding back because of this list? If so, where? Which item on the list feels most potent? Write it down in your workbook or a journal. Then, write down one way this perceived problem or flaw has been a gift or blessing in some way. It doesn't matter how small or insignificant the silver lining seems. Prepare to diffuse this pain point further in the pages that follow.

Part One: Aware

"Change as a choice requires you to be aware of your automatic programs and consciously decide not to go unconscious again."

—Dr. Joe Dispenza

Chapter 1

The Power of Intention

"The principle of intention is literally what saved and changed the trajectory of my life."

—Oprah Winfrey

The energy and focus we put into our thoughts, desires, and intentions shape our reality. The law of intention suggests that when we set clear and positive intentions, the universe and higher consciousness respond by aligning circumstances and opportunities to help us achieve those intentions.

Intention is the precursor to strategy, planning, goals, and targets. It effectively informs our thoughts and perceptions, our feelings, our actions, and our results. Like an adventurer's compass that helps to correct and stay on course, so too does intention help us navigate our daily lives in alignment and integrity. That's why we begin here.

My friend Sandy Critides introduced me to the power of mindful intention. Before we'd host or attend an event together, she'd ask me what my intention was—what I wanted to contribute, how I wanted to feel and show up energetically, and what I wanted to gain from being there. Usually, my intentions unfolded as desired. Impressed with the effective simplicity of this practice, I quickly began to apply mindful intention to other areas of my life. I'd ask myself questions like, *What is my intention for this coaching call? What is my intention for this workout?* What I intended was typically what transpired. The beauty of this simple practice is that it is accessible to everyone, anytime.

Often, simple shifts like this create the biggest impact. Choosing a word of the year is an example. The first time I chose a word of the year and focused on it, I was coming off a rough first year of entrepreneurship. When I created my first business from the ground up, I squandered precious financial resources and wasn't focused on maintaining harmony at home or anywhere else. I took a great deal for granted. Fortunately, I regained consciousness in time to make the necessary changes.

A guiding light in that process of reflection and reclamation was my intentional word of the year, *stewardship.* Stewardship is defined as *the careful and responsible management of something entrusted to one's care.*[1] This word encompassed everything: my beautiful family, my natural gifts and talents, finances, and opportunities.

By making *stewardship* my intention, I created space to assess and consciously decide before acting. For example, when it came time to invest in my next business, this intentionality made me pause and ask myself, *Am I being a good steward of resources by moving forward with this opportunity?* With family, it often showed up like, *If I intend to be a good steward of this child in my care, is the best thing I can do right now spending quality time with my daughter, or is it working longer, even though work can wait?* At home, the intention of stewardship often looked like getting into a rhythm of tidiness or cooking more often. Physically, it got me into the gym and out on walks more than ever before.

One word backed with strong intention and emotional charge created more presence and spaciousness in my life than any meditation or spiritual practice ever had.

This is the premise this book rests on. With heartful intention to embody and act as your Higher Self, you will create the spaciousness from which you can consciously create the life of your choosing.

Intention is the primer. It keeps us anchored to our *why* for doing anything, which is extraordinarily helpful in a world where we are pummeled with stimuli and distractions 24/7. If you feel like a rolling stone and can't seem to stay in one place long enough to gather the moss you so desire, maybe some focused intention is all that's needed.

Our brains are incredibly powerful. When we focus the power of our minds in alignment with strong, heartfelt emotion, we begin to 3D print our thoughts into reality. You've experienced this firsthand, consciously or not, and for better or worse. Can you think of a person, circumstance, experience, or object you've brought into your reality simply because you were intentional and focused on doing so? Maybe it was the home you live in, your partner, the dream job or business you're in, or the car you drive. If no examples come to mind, that's okay too. Silently or aloud, say this to yourself right now: *Show me evidence that my intentions and focus create my reality.* And be ready to take note because the evidence *will* present itself. (You'll learn why and how in Chapter 6.)

You may intuitively know the power of intention *and* appreciate proof when it's available. A study conducted at the HeartMath Institute provides such proof, beautifully illustrating the power of intention. The study aimed to explore the impact of human intentionality on DNA structure by involving participants trained in HeartMath techniques.[2] These techniques focus on generating heart coherence through positive emotions like love and appreciation.

Heart coherence is defined as a state in which the heart, mind, and emotions operate harmoniously. In this state, the heart's rhythm exhibits a smooth, wave-like pattern, indicating that the body's systems are working together efficiently and in sync. Heart coherence is often measured using heart rate variability (HRV), the variation in time between each heartbeat. The higher the HRV, the higher the coherence levels, associated with improved cognitive performance, emotional stability, and overall well-being.

The study was designed to test whether individuals, while in a state of heart coherence, could intentionally alter the conformation of DNA—specifically, to wind or unwind its structure. The participants held a beaker containing a small, sealed test tube of DNA. They held the beaker for two minutes while generating feelings of love and appreciation and focusing their intention on either winding or unwinding the DNA. Participants who generated high levels of heart coherence while intending to change the DNA showed significant alterations in DNA conformation. In some cases, changes of up to 25 percent were observed! The control group participants did the same, but these participants were not trained in HeartMath techniques. Despite all other variables being equal, the DNA the control group participants held showed no significant changes in conformation.

The *only* difference between the two groups was that one was trained to get their hearts (emotions) and minds (intentional thoughts) into agreement or coherence, while the other group was not. This created incoherence, preventing the control group from manifesting significant changes in the DNA. Think about the implications of this for a moment. How often have we done something when our heart wasn't in it? Usually, this looks like "should-ing" on ourselves. *I should do this; I should do that.* It also looks like saying yes out of obligation. When our emotions and cognition aren't aligned, it creates internal conflict and incoherence. It also makes our actions less effective—and likely more difficult.

Can you remember a time when your heart and mind disagreed? Did the related actions you took feel difficult and laborious? Now think about something both your heart and mind were fully in agreement on. Whatever you did while in this state, did it flow and feel easy?

Back to the HeartMath study for a moment. Another key finding happened when researchers had participants do the experiment *nonlocally.* Some participants maintained heart coherence and their intention to change the DNA while located half a mile from the DNA sample. *Despite the distance, significant changes in DNA conformation were observed!* This suggests that the effects on the DNA were not solely due to direct physical contact with the sample and could be achieved through focused intention alone, even from a distance.

It's mind-blowing, right? This is the power of the quantum field at work! We'll explore the quantum more in Chapter 10. Until then, let this remind you of what's possible with aligned intentions and emotional states. How can this change your life and the world?

What could you create in your lived experience if you consistently aligned your heart and mind? The law of mirroring states that external events, circumstances, and people we encounter reflect our inner state, thoughts, and emotions. "As within, so without." (More on this in Chapter 7.) If you want to change the world, it's an inside job. And it starts with aligned, heartfelt intention.

FAITH

When our logical mind resists or doesn't believe what we feel and know in our heart, the solution is shifting to faith: complete trust and the firm belief in something for which there is no proof.[3]

Relative to my heart, my mind is easy to change. The heart is the seat of the soul, and it knows the truth. There's a saying, "The heart wants what it wants," but I'd argue this is the egoic mind playing a clever trick to disguise itself. When I look back on "heartbreaks," I can see that calling them "ego breaks" would be far more accurate. Our souls and hearts know every meeting between persons aids both in their respective and collective evolutions. Sometimes, that meeting will last a lifetime. Often, it won't. But when there's love between people, it's eternal. The heart and soul know this. Only the ego believes in the finite. We often say someone has a special place in our hearts after they're no longer in our lives. I believe they *do*, and that if we can let that be enough—for everything that leaves our orbit (jobs, homes, possessions, money, people)—we can solve much of our inner turmoil.

This is where faith comes in. Can you surrender your attachments to a particular outcome, person, or possession and have complete trust that it will work out for your benefit and the highest good of all? This can be an extremely foreign and uncomfortable feeling for those who love control. (And yes, I'm speaking from experience.) Luckily, our minds are malleable. Thanks to neuroplasticity, we can train, change, and rewire our brains to think in a way that is more supportive and aligned with the life and experiences we desire.

What about those times when our heart and mind disagree, and our mind wins the argument? Faith comes in clutch then too. This is usually when we make a mess of things or learn a lesson the hard way. I seem to have an affinity for this type of learning. But there's always a silver lining and a seed of opportunity if only we can hold the faith that it's so.

BE HER NOW EXERCISE:

Before you go on, take a moment to think about the intentions you hold for your life. If that feels too big, how about the intention(s) for today, this next week, month, or year? Or your intentions for reading this book? Write them down and be as detailed or brief as you'd like. This will be an anchor to return to throughout the process of meeting your Higher Self.

BE HER NOW REFLECTION:

What's something you've lost, the absence of which turned out to be a blessing? Is there something you don't currently have in your life but deeply desire? Have you set an intention and directed your focus to it? How can you plug in faith and trust in the timing? How can you feel gratitude as if it's already happened?

Chapter 2

The Slow and Steady Strategy

"In the confrontation between the stream and the rock, the stream always wins, not through strength but by perseverance."

—H. Jackson Brown Jr.

One of my favorite childhood stories perfectly illustrates the power of consistent, small habits: Aesop's children's fable, *The Tortoise and The Hare*. Here's the gist if it's been a few years since you read it. The hare is arrogant, always bragging about his speed. Growing tired of this, the tortoise challenges him to a race. With cockiness, the hare accepts. The race begins, and the hare takes off. He gains such a commanding lead that he stops to take a nap ... before the finish line. Meanwhile, the tortoise continues, slow, steady, and consistent. He passes a peacefully sleeping hare on his way to the finish line. The hare eventually wakes up, but it's too late to catch up and overtake the tortoise, and the tortoise wins. I imagine him enjoying peace and quiet now that he's taken the hare down a notch.

Being like the tortoise is how you become your Higher Self. It's slow and steady, letting the compounding power of habits take you there slowly at first, then more rapidly as momentum builds. This may not be as exciting or flashy as the flair with which the hare bolted off and the subsequent franticness of trying to catch up and win. But winning is pretty damn exciting too. Slow and steady is how we win the game of life.

It's said that compounding interest is the eighth wonder of the world. Compounding interest usually refers to money earning interest, but it also applies to personal growth. Small, consistent habits compound into *huge* results.

We get a little better through every seemingly insignificant action that aligns with our intentions. We trust and like ourselves a little more. Our capacity expands. If we continue stacking these little wins, before long, we'll have made significant progress. And that improved version of us can hold more than we could when we started. Our new habits become automatic if we consistently stick to these small actions. Our decision fatigue over the daily minutiae begins to fade away. We can now handle more and more of what we desire, and we trust our ability to steward this new abundance. At this point, our growth isn't linear—it's exponential.

There is another fable to share here—one that sold me on this concept. The story goes that a dying father tells his twin sons they must choose their inheritance. The choices are $1,000,000 in cash or a purse with one cent. But there's one catch: the value of the purse with the penny will double daily until the money is withdrawn. When I read this, I thought the answer was obvious. Before you read on, which would you choose? Go with your first answer.

One twin picks the million dollars, and one picks the purse with the penny. The twin who chooses the million blows it, but the part of the story that captivates me is the math on the purse with daily doubling value. If you start with a penny and double its total compounded value daily, at the end of thirty days, you will have $5,368,709.12. That doesn't even seem possible, does it? But, the math is mathing. See Figure 2.1 below.

Day	Value ($)	Day	Value ($)
1	.01	16	327.68
2	.02	17	655.36
3	.04	18	1,310.72
4	.08	19	2,621.44
5	.16	20	5,242.88
6	.32	21	10,485.76
7	.64	22	20,971.52
8	1.28	23	41,943.04
9	2.56	24	83,886.08
10	5.12	25	167,772.16
11	10.24	26	335,544.32
12	20.48	27	671,088.64
13	40.96	28	1,342,177.28
14	81.92	29	2,684,354.56
15	163.84	30	5,368,709.12

Figure 2.1: The incredible value of a penny if left to compound 100 percent daily over thirty days.

Were you as shocked as I was that such an insignificant amount of money could grow to such a huge amount so quickly? And look, I know there is no 100 percent interest rate with daily compounding available anywhere. It's also unreasonable and unrealistic for a person to double their ability or capacity every day. But now that you know what's possible with compounding— how an insignificant penny can balloon to over $5 million in a month—what if we take this same principle but make the growth ultra-conservative? Like, standard savings account conservative. A standard savings account earns about 0.5 percent interest. What if you set a baseline to improve yourself by half of 1 percent daily? That's so marginal you wouldn't even notice it. Most days, you'd probably do more with little to no effort. But let's say you stick to the baseline of 0.5 percent. If you improve yourself by 0.5 percent every day, at the end of the year, you'll be 6.17 times better than you are today.[4] I don't know about you, but I'm living a much richer life in every sense if I 6x my current state! The incredible part about growth compounding at such a low rate is that it happens so gradually that it's not a shake-up or shock to your system. Gradual success is a blessing because it allows you to adapt and grow comfortable, making you far less likely to sabotage your gains. Unfortunately, we've been conditioned to think small doesn't matter.

I also want to acknowledge that many little things are always vying for our attention. Acting as if every single one needs to be acted on and paid attention to is not what I'm advocating here. Discernment is critical, yet I still encourage you to begin noting the little things and how much some of them matter and may move the needle. (To give you a few quick examples, unloading the dishwasher first thing in the morning, making the bed before I begin working, or getting five minutes of sunlight after a stretch at the computer are *tiny* shifts that always make an outsized impact on my entire day.)

Now for some real talk. We will never experience exponential growth with ease if we continue to favor the quick fixes and instant gratification that so many of us (including me) have grown accustomed to. Maybe you can relate to some of the following tendencies.

Throughout my life, I have been praised and rewarded for big, bold action. Especially for things that came to me easily, like speed did to the hare. Like the hare, I'm wired to go hard and then nap—literally and metaphorically. For example, school wasn't particularly challenging for me. Why study consistently when I could have fun and do other things with that time and cram before a test, eking out a good grade? Why tidy up my room each day when I could clean up a big mess in a whirling dervish when my parents (or I) finally couldn't stand it any longer? Why make the number of consistent sales calls a day when I could take it easy-ish, focus on a couple of big accounts, and leverage end-of-quarter or end-of-year pricing (and usually a frantic calling blitz) to surpass my quota? I had mastered flexing on whatever came my way—which surely has its upsides. But this was *terrible* for teaching me consistency or discipline. If you tend to procrastinate and do this, you might even get a thrill from it. I know I did.

Finally, I got right-sized like the hare. Big, bold, fast, and inconsistent actions don't work in entrepreneurship. Maybe in the short term, but not in the long term. Slow and steady win the race in business and life, and I have had to eat *a lot* of humble pie since becoming a "corporate dropout" to finally figure that out.

Many of us approach our health the same way. I'm a millennial born in 1985, the height of diet culture in America. In my teens and twenties, I favored crash diets, two-a-day workouts, and the Cabbage Soup Diet to prep for a beach vacation instead of making consistent and simple lifestyle changes.

Can you relate to any of these behaviors? If so, you know from experience that a roller coaster is fun to ride for a little while, but stay on too long, and you'll throw up, need a chiropractor, or both. Living your life through big, bold, and inconsistent actions is the same. It became exhausting, and I got sick of it! Have you finally hit *your* limit? Are you sick of your own shit yet? If so, good! That means you're ready to upgrade your identity and level up!

Remember, *we are going for results that last, not results that are fast.* Although I promise you *will* see small changes fast!

In the next chapter, we'll dive into this further, as well as some of the modern conditioning that's keeping us small. But first, let's take a moment to reflect and get into action.

BE HER NOW REFLECTION:

Where in your life have you been more focused on speed and quick fixes than creating simple consistency? Can you pinpoint where this tendency started for you?

BE HER NOW EXERCISE:

What is *one* small, seemingly insignificant action you can take today? Is it making your bed? Drinking one more glass of water? Remembering to take your vitamins? Think small. After you do it, thank yourself, and *relish in feeling good about it.* (More to come later on why feeling good makes habits stick.)

Chapter 3

All-or-Nothing Is Your Achilles Heel

"Perfectionism is not a quest for the best. It is a pursuit of the worst in ourselves, the part that tells us that nothing we do will ever be good enough—that we should try again."

—Julia Cameron

"Go big or go home" and all-or-nothing mentalities are perfectionism in disguise. They're keeping us stuck and holding us back more than we realize.

Maybe it's being American and the culture in the United States, but there is a general sense that bigger is better. Back to the penny in the purse example from the last chapter. How often have you not done something because it seemed too small and insignificant to make a difference? Or because it seemed too easy, and something must feel hard for it to count? If I had a dollar for every time I've *not* done something because it was too small or too easy, I'd have enough money to play Oprah and gift a car to each of you.

While I believe human beings are drawn to continuous expansion, we usually go about it incorrectly. We feel like the way to go big is to, well ... go big. To do something extreme, something we must muster up the courage for, something that might take a ton of time and resources. And if it doesn't pay off (it often doesn't), we're left burnt out, embarrassed, and less resourced than before. Things not working is part of the human experience, but where did we get the idea that we must do (and fail) on a grand scale? How can we make the shift from grand to granular?

I'll tell you another reason I loathe this "go big" mindset, which I'm still working to unwind. When we do everything big, it stops being fun. If there's pressure for something to be perfect, a huge hit, or an overnight success, it becomes a joy vampire. Sometimes pressure is exciting. Other times it creates an explosion. (If you have an Instant Pot, you may have experienced this firsthand.) Maybe it's because I'm getting older, but more and more, I find the little things bring me the most joy. They don't come with pressure or a big price tag, and they're sustainable too.

Another way this vein of thinking bigger is better can show up is when we don't pursue an experience or opportunity because we don't feel qualified. This is especially pervasive among women. Hewlett-Packard (HP) conducted an internal study, which found that men would apply for a promotion when they believed they could meet 60 percent of the job requirements. Meanwhile, women would apply when they met *all* of the qualifications. Yes—100 percent of them![5] And look, this isn't just women holding ourselves back. There's gender bias at play here too. Men tend to be evaluated on future potential, while women are evaluated more heavily on past performance.[6] These reflect broader issues related to confidence, impostor syndrome, and societal expectations. But let's not lose the plot.

Applying this HP study to how we live our lives is painting with a broad brush, and I realize that. But I see this readiness waiting game in myself and talented women I admire and respect. I don't see my male friends sidelining themselves like this. Women tend to wait until we are fully ready and completely qualified, while men trust they can figure it out. We, too, can figure it out! What if we went for it when we were 60 percent ready, like our male counterparts? Or 75 percent? Even 95 percent would be an improvement! Until we make a different choice and start when we don't feel prepared or qualified, this perfectionist thinking will hold us back, collectively and individually.

High-achieving women can feel we need to be near-perfect (or working toward it) to be worthy of our desired results. Hell, I'm even walking that line with this book title, aren't I? Many of us feel if we aren't immediately excelling in an endeavor, something must be wrong with us or perhaps it's not worth doing. The go big or go home mentality is a way of putting a stake in the ground. A defense mechanism of sorts, showing how committed and serious we are to make up for and protect against any possible shortcomings. It protects us, as if to say, *Well, it didn't work out, but look how hard she tried! She gets an A for effort!* But this is exhausting and wasting our potential. We are worthy, no matter the outcome.

I don't want to diminish these feelings of needing to go above and beyond, though. They're valid. There's a lot of history that has shaped our collective subconscious that reinforces women's feelings of inadequacy and powerlessness.

For example, we couldn't get a business loan without a male cosigner until 1988.[7] Our husbands or male relatives could lock us in a sanatorium or mental institution without cause or our consent if we became inconvenient for any reason. (It didn't become illegal to confine a non-dangerous individual to a mental institution without due process of law until 1975![8]) And look what happened to Britney Spears. Her freedom was taken from her for over a decade in a conservatorship by her father. I don't share these examples to foster victimhood or to depress you. I share them as a reminder that there is nothing wrong with you for feeling like you need to check every box. Recent history shows why trying to be perfect and pleasing was a great strategy for survival. But how long are we willing to let the past shape our future?

BE HER NOW REFLECTION:

Do a quick check-in with yourself.

- Do you relate to not starting something until you're ready?
- Do you feel worthy to receive abundance, recognition, or success even if you haven't checked all the arbitrary boxes? (Whose boxes are they, anyway?)
- Are you still equating your worth with your contributions and achievements?
- If you're being really honest, is there collective or generational trauma keeping you in a state of people-pleasing and perfectionism as a protection mechanism?

If you like to clear your head through movement, breath, or journaling, this might be a good time to take a beat before you continue. Confronting these patterns is called "doing the work" for a reason! Celebrate your bravery in doing so.

Beyond historical reasons, there are a myriad of factors that contribute to women's struggles with all-or-nothing perfectionist tendencies. (And yes, being judged on past performance rather than our future potential doesn't help.) Check out the list below and note how many resonate with your own lived experience.

- In college, a female professor told the women in our class that to excel in most workplace settings, we'd need to be twice as good as our male peers. Other marginalized people often have this experience too. Have you ever felt you needed to be better than or work harder than others to gain recognition or career advancement?
- As women, we may be more prone to a fear of negative evaluation or criticism, leading us to strive for perfection to avoid criticism or judgment from others. This is rooted in "good girl syndrome" and people-pleasing, which are books unto themselves.
- Some of us set exceptionally high standards for ourselves due to personal expectations or external pressures, such as parental or societal expectations. These pressures are often more pronounced for eldest children and children of immigrants. (I can vouch for both.) And, of course, there's the accompanying guilt and shame when we don't surpass these lofty and often unrealistic expectations.

- We may feel we have less control over certain aspects of our lives, leading us to focus intensely on areas we believe we can control, such as our performance and appearance. Cultural and media influences often perpetuate the idea of the "perfect woman" regarding appearance, behavior, and success, leading to more unrealistic expectations.
- Societal gender norms may reinforce the idea that we should excel in all areas of life, including work, relationships, and appearance. Many moms are trying to unwind the notion that we ought to work as if we don't have children and mother as if we don't work.
- In the age of the internet with aesthetically pleasing Instagram feeds, misleading highlight reels, and trolls in the comments, we can feel pressure in several areas. To strive for a rocking body and to look stylish, on-trend, and effortlessly put together. To keep our house tidy, with decor worthy of an *Architectural Digest* spread. To cook organic, non-processed dinners for our families as many nights a week as possible. With porn readily available in a couple of clicks, we'd better keep our husbands satisfied too. And it's not that we don't love sex; we're just *tired* from all the above and more.

These are some of the reasons why we burn out, throw up our hands, and lose our spark. We are really good at spinning many plates, but when was the last time you stopped to see how many you've picked up and accumulated? You might be spinning the whole china cabinet! It's time to put some of them down. (By the way, did you consciously choose these plates? How many actually belong to you?)

BE HER NOW REFLECTION:

If you're a woman, ask yourself honestly: How much of this chapter has resonated with you? What expectations can you begin to remove and shed? How can you begin to see yourself as worthy and enough just as you are? (If you have a male partner, ask him the questions below.)

If you're a man, how has reading this chapter made you feel? What expectations do you unconsciously hold around women that reinforce the status quo? How can you support the women in your life to affirm their inherent worthiness? (If you have a female partner, ask her the questions above.)

The irony in perfectionism is that often, as we "go big or go home," we secretly hold a piece of ourselves and our effort back. That way, if our pursuit or endeavor fails, we have a reason why it did, and we can protect our egos.

I love the idea of "leaving it all on the field" or giving it everything you've got, but there are so many times I have purposely *not* done this. If I tied my worth to my success and gave something my all, and it failed or flopped or wasn't deemed good enough, then as an extension, *I would not be good enough.* And when we're operating from a place of perfectionism, *identifying with our doing,* giving something a wholehearted effort is risky. If we can create distance between our identity and our production, we are liberated to go all in where we want to.

YOU AREN'T FEDEX—AND YOU CAN'T OVERNIGHT IT

Overnight success is a pervasive myth that many of us latch onto when it comes to personal change or business. When we see the meteoric rise of another, we probably don't see the failures and work that happened for years in the dark. We only notice when they've crossed the tipping point and gained our attention. Of course, we know the truth: persistence and consistency win the day and create "overnight" success.

The world's first self-made female millionaire is a great example.[9] Madam C. J. Walker was an African American entrepreneur, inventor, and philanthropist. Through her business, Madam C. J. Walker Manufacturing Company, she made her fortune by developing and marketing a line of cosmetics and hair care products for Black women.

Walker had a difficult early life, working in various jobs before finding her way in the beauty industry. She struggled with hair loss from a scalp condition, which led her to experiment with different hair care treatments and products. After much trial and error, she developed a product that promoted hair growth.

Starting with door-to-door sales, she gradually built up a thriving business that included a factory, a beauty school, and a team of trained sales beauticians.[10] Walker's persistent and consistent work, done away from the limelight, laid the foundation for her success long before the public became aware of her achievements. Her story is a testament that "overnight success" results from many years building in the dark.

Critical to Walker's and *any* success is a willingness to keep trying, "failing," and noting what works and what doesn't. In fact, we will take this same approach when we jump into habit design in Chapter 18. The good news is it probably won't take many attempts to get your ideal habits right.

As we continue this journey together, remember:

We live in the age of Amazon Prime. We can instantly stream entertainment on Netflix with no commercials. Thanks to DoorDash, those of us in urban areas can get food delivered to our homes from our favorite restaurants in thirty minutes— sometimes less. We can listen to Taylor Swift's new album on Spotify the day it's released. The days of going to the store to buy a CD and hoping it hasn't sold out are long gone. I'm old enough to remember calling the radio station to request a song and then waiting for it to (hopefully) come on! While these technological advancements have many benefits, we've grown accustomed to instant gratification. We also see the highlight reels on social media that lead us to compare our Chapter 1 to someone else's Chapter 10 ... of their second book. Then we wonder what we're doing wrong not to make five figures or more the first months we're in business.

It's easy to fall into the trap of expecting instant (unrealistic) results in our habits, lives, and businesses. This is why we try to go big, feel we've failed when it doesn't happen immediately, and ultimately quit. These perceived "failures" can keep us out of the game for a while, and sometimes they sideline us for good.

But *small* is mighty. Yes, results from consistency can take time, but they're long-lasting too. Grandiose to granular wins the day.

Continuous improvement is better than delayed perfection. It's exactly what will unlock levels of self-trust and confidence that you never knew were possible. We've been trying to be the hare even though we know the tortoise wins. Get ready to embrace your inner tortoise and the victory that comes with it.

If you struggle with all-or-nothing thinking and wonder why you can't seem to give it a go when it comes to your dreams or living a life in alignment with the authentic version of you, remember these wise words from Brené Brown: "Perfectionism is a twenty-ton shield that we lug around thinking it will protect us when, in fact, it's the thing that's really preventing us from taking flight."

Time to set down that heavy shield, spread your wings, and fly. That's where we're heading next—and how you can make it simple.

BE HER NOW REFLECTION:

Approach this question with curiosity and love. Leave your judgment at the door. Where are you holding yourself back *right now* because you're aiming for a level of perfection?

Did you try performing a small behavior from the last chapter that you've been wanting to do? If so, how did it make you feel? If not, how does *that* make you feel? Emotions help us wire in new behaviors as habits, so really lean into *small* actions that don't take much time and that make you feel awesome.

Chapter 4

Keep It Simple

"The journey of a thousand miles begins with a single step."

—Lao Tzu

ONE STEP AT A TIME

Standing at the bottom of several flights of stairs at the Andaz Hotel in Maui, I noticed a sign etched in stone with the above Lao Tzu quote. After I read it, the number of stairs before me didn't seem so daunting. I just needed to take it one step at a time.

The same is true of our journey to becoming our Higher Self. Many of us won't take that first step because the distance between where we are now and where we want to go is so vast it's downright terrifying. I've been caught in this trap before. But the beauty of this process is just that—the process itself. Just do the next right thing. And take a moment to appreciate how far you've already come!

High-achieving go-getters like us can feel unhappy because we tend to measure progress in a way that makes us feel bad. We measure ourselves against our ideal, which becomes problematic since our ideal evolves and changes as we do. It'd be like walking toward the horizon, expecting to arrive at the horizon as if it were a static point. That doesn't work because the horizon moves as we do. It's the same reason chasing a dangled carrot is a losing battle. Under this paradigm of measuring ourselves against our future, we never get closer.

What if instead, we measured our current selves by how far we've come? For one, this provides an accurate metric. You know where you started, and you know where you are. On the other hand, becoming your Higher Self may require some detours or take more time than expected. That can be frustrating. Measuring ourselves against our progress makes us feel good and grateful. It also keeps us focused on our continual growth—encouraging us to higher levels of attainment and a greater sense of possibility. This is also why the fifth stage of the *Higher Self Habits* method, Ascend and Amplify, is critical. It reminds you to stop and note the new level you just unlocked. From there, you'll gain awareness of what's next and within your reach, but not before you pause to rest and marvel at your progress. Celebrating growth is a key component of lasting transformation.

Another possible reason you haven't taken it to the next level could be you're overwhelmed by where you are now. Like how the saying "more money, more problems" can provide a balm to keep someone content with being broke. It makes you stop and think, *I don't want more! I can barely handle what I have now! I'll just stick with these feelings of inadequacy and mediocrity.* But just like more money, more of the *right* habits can solve problems. And, *the habits that are right for you* will serve as expanders. They reduce or eliminate decision fatigue and overwhelm. They open our capacity to hold and handle more. Habits and structure are the antidote to feeling as if we're drowning. Stick with me, and I'll prove it to you.

MEET CLARITY, YOUR NEW BFF

Confused people do nothing, so let's bring clarity to your entire habits journey right now with three principles, synthesized from two of the all-time bestselling habits books: *The 7 Habits of Highly Effective People* by Stephen Covey and *High Performance Habits*[11] by Brendon Burchard.

Principle 1: Be proactive—as much and as often as possible.

When I'm overwhelmed, it's always because I'm reacting or because I've let too much pile up. Usually, that pileup or the fire that needs to be put out comes with urgency. Franticness usually ensues. Shifting to proactivity brings ease and calm. Your responsibilities don't disappear, but you handle them differently.

Becky is a client in one of my programs. On one of our group coaching calls, she shared a profound insight about watering houseplants that sums this up perfectly. When you proactively water your plants, you feel proud. When you think about watering them but don't, in a few days they start to wilt. Now you need to water them reactively. This brings relief, but not pride. Shame might tag along too, as a byproduct of "should-ing" on yourself. It might sound something like, *I should have watered my fiddle leaf fig when I remembered. Now it looks like it's knocking on death's door.* Remember it like this: *Proactivity* brings *pride. Reactivity* brings *relief.* And reactivity usually involves *should-ing* on yourself, which brings *shame.*

Remember, we're ascending to a higher level—and we do that by feeling good!

When we're operating from a deficit and playing catch up, the idea of being proactive can feel impossible. If you're there right now, take a quick assessment. What *actually* needs to be done? What can be deleted? What can be delegated? What can be deferred to a later date without much fuss?

If you've got more on your plate that you can handle after delegating, deleting, and deferring, I have one more for you. Start declining. What do you need to say no to? Or maybe it isn't a no, but a *not right now*. What have you said yes to that you need to decline? I know letting people down and going back on commitments feels terrible, but be honest and tell them why. In my experience when I've done this, people have appreciated the transparency. Sometimes it's given them the permission they needed to do the same. And look, a lot of the shit piled on your plate doesn't need to be done, anyway.

When narrowing in on what you *do* need to do, it turns out there are better times for certain tasks, the knowledge of which has changed my life. Enter, cycle syncing. If you're a woman in her menstruating years and haven't heard of this, without exaggeration, I'm about to change your life with this concept. I learned about cycle syncing at the ripe age of thirty-six, but as with most things, better late than never.

The basic premise of cycle syncing is that women function on a twenty-eight-day hormone cycle while men function on a twenty-four-hour cycle. No surprise, our modern world was built by, around, and arguably for men. But we can recover the power of our cycles by syncing the four different phases to our various responsibilities. This, in turn, makes everything we do easier to execute, since each phase parallels a season and is ideal for certain tasks and activities:

1. Menstrual: resting, reflecting recharging (winter)
2. Follicular: planning, preparing, ideating, creating (spring)
3. Ovulatory: socializing, communicating, selling (summer)
4. Luteal: doing admin and detail-oriented activities; getting projects done (fall)

Can you imagine how much your life would flow (pun intended) if you began to proactively shift your schedule to align with your cycle? And since most of us have never done this, even a tiny shift will yield results.

Here's how I do this. Go to whatever calendar you use to run your life, whether it's Google, Outlook, or a paper one. Make note of the phases of your cycle and mark the dates you're expecting them. (If you're unsure of your cycle phases, MyFlo is my cycle-tracking app of choice.) Make each phase a repeating event based on the length of your cycle. Adjust as needed, and voilà! Sometimes, we need to do something that's not ideal for a given phase, like going to an event the day we start our period. It won't be perfect, and we're done with perfection anyway, remember? Even with hiccups, adding the phases to my calendar has made a significant difference in creating ease and has made it much easier to plan accordingly where possible.

The basics of cycle syncing also provide flexible guidelines for habits. As you create menus of supportive habits later in this book, cycle syncing can guide which behavior is best based on how you feel and your current cycle phase.

If this concept intrigues you, you'll be thrilled to learn that specific foods can be incorporated into each phase, as well as different optimal forms of exercise. That level of depth is better explored in books dedicated to the subject, which you can find in the suggested reading list in the back of this book and at alessiacitro.com/book.

Rounding out *Principle 1: Be Proactive*, there's a mantra I invite you to play with that has improved my life a great deal.

Do now what you'll be grateful for later. (Later might mean an hour from now or tomorrow—not some far-flung date.)

Besides making my days run smoother, this advice has even made my marriage happier. For example, I'm the messier one in my marriage, and my husband cannot stand clutter. It literally affects his mental state. Despite knowing this, I would let dishes pile up in the sink. Jeff is more than happy to share the workload around the house and does so without being asked, but this behavior of mine drove him nuts. So, I made one change so simple it sounds insignificant, like the penny in the purse. I began running the dishwasher before bed, emptying it first thing in the morning, and putting the dishes straight into the dishwasher throughout the day. That's it! This takes a small investment of time, and I always thank myself for doing it. The cumulative effect of being proactive in this way removed the stressor created by the mess. It reinforced the type of partner, housekeeper, and person I want to be. My confidence and capacity expanded through this simple behavior change. The gravy is that it makes my husband feel happy and peaceful in the process, which makes me feel good too. Most tiny changes like this have a comparable ripple effect that will make you wonder why you didn't start sooner.

BE HER NOW REFLECTION:

Where can you be more proactive in your life? (Hint: It's probably the stuff you're dreading.)

Being proactive also means planning ahead, which leads to the second principle.

Principle 2: Get clear on your desired goal or aspiration and start with that end in mind.

This principle is critical. It's why I had you set an intention in the very beginning of the book. Good questions to ask to narrow in on your true desires are:

- What's actually important to me?
- Who do I want to become?
- How would becoming that version of myself benefit me—emotionally, spiritually, mentally, physically, and financially?
- How would it benefit the people I love, my community, and even society at large?
- Why does any of this matter to me?

Once you're clear on the who, what, why, and how, you can begin to align with your values and true priorities.

BE HER NOW EXERCISE:

What is the aspiration or goal that initially came to mind as you read this section? Take a moment to write it down—either in this book, a journal, or your companion workbook.

Principle 3: Put first things first.

As Covey famously said, "The main thing is to let the main thing be the main thing."[12]

You might be thinking, *How am I supposed to do that when I have varied interests, obligations, and responsibilities?* Or maybe that's my ADHD and proclivity toward shiny objects and mental squirrels projecting on you. Either way, it's worth exploring.

We discussed in *Principle 1: Be Proactive*, how we must begin deleting, delegating, deferring, and declining. But that doesn't always work for our deeply ingrained interests. Figure 4.1 (which can be downloaded in color for free at alessiacitro. com/book) illustrates my decision-making process in a visual flow chart format. This is how I decide where to focus my time.

Before you start the flow, what is a task or obligation that consumes a lot of your time or energy? Keep it in mind.

Now, recall the goal or aspiration you wrote down for *Principle 2* and put the above task or obligation through the flow below, leaving room for nuance and necessary parsing out.

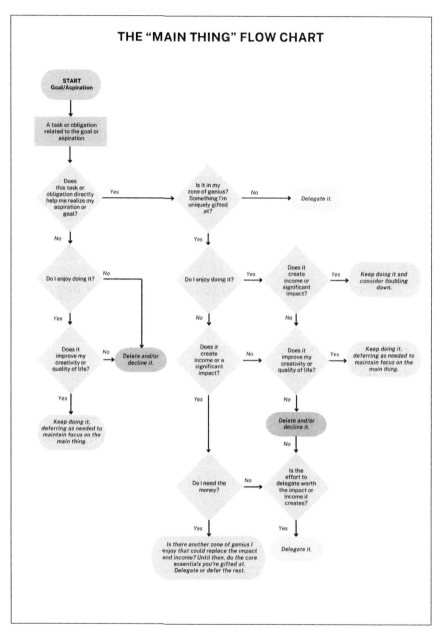

Figure 4.1: A decision tree to help keep the main thing, the main thing.

The above isn't foolproof, but it's a start. An example I put through this flow, with a lot of nuance, is answering emails. My inbox management has a lot of room for improvement. No matter what I do or what methods I put in place, I struggle to stay on top of it. Emails pile up faster than I can delete or reply to them. While there are some that I need to handle, the reality is that most of my inbox doesn't require me or the information exclusively housed in my brain. Here's what the flow looked like as I went through it over two rounds, parsing out the important emails from the junk.

Goal and aspiration: To move my business forward and build relationships.

Task or obligation: Respond to important emails in a timely manner.

- *Does this task or obligation directly help me realize my aspiration or goal?* Yes.
- *Is it in my zone of genius—something I'm uniquely gifted at?* Yes, no one else can answer these, for now.
- *Do I enjoy doing it?* Usually, yes. When I don't, it's because it's admin, like providing deliverables or following up on something that needs to get done but doesn't move the needle.
- *Does it create income or a significant impact?* If it's an email with a potential partner or client, yes.
- *My result*: Keep doing it and consider doubling down. (Remember, this is just for important emails that only I can do.)

How about for the task of cleaning my inbox of junk mail and staying up to date with other communication?

- *Does this task or obligation directly help me realize my aspiration or goal?* A gray area ... but overall, no.
- *Do I enjoy doing it?* Absolutely not. I detest it.
- *Does it improve my creativity or quality of life?* Definitely not, unless it's entertaining or crucially informative.
- *My result:* Delete or decline it.

Here's where discernment comes in. Email isn't going anywhere. What steps can I take to delete or decline anything that isn't moving me toward my goal? This might look like mass deleting or unsubscribing. It might mean signing up for things with a junk email I don't need to check. It might mean delegating the rest to a virtual assistant. Regardless, this flow of questioning will illuminate what you'd benefit from spending time on, and which tasks are time, energy, or creativity vampires.

Summing it up, keeping the main thing the main thing is to keep your eye on the prize. If something doesn't help achieve your aspiration, make money, energize you, enhance your creativity, improve your life, or bring you joy, it's time to dump it.

Of course, this is all easier said than done. It can be difficult to maintain focus on key priorities when we are constantly bombarded. But that's where intention and mission come in. Intention serves as an anchor. It keeps us grounded and moored to what we said we wanted. It's okay to change our minds, but at least know what you're pivoting to and why. Meanwhile, our mission functions a lot like GPS. We may change the route or means of getting to our destination, but keeping the destination front and center keeps us headed in the right direction.

So, by all means—indulge in your interests. Cultivate hobbies. Incorporate variety. Detours can enhance and make any trip more fun, so long as they're not dangerous and we can still get back to the main road.

In Chapter 8, we'll discuss keeping your big vision at the forefront of your mind. Until then, I invite you to do the exercises below, especially the bonus: writing a personal mission statement.[13]

We've heard of businesses having mission statements, but you probably haven't heard of a *person* having one. I certainly hadn't! But it's brilliant. How can we live a life of purpose if we haven't taken the time to deeply consider our mission and orient our actions to it? And I'm not talking about some boilerplate corporate garbage that checks a box. *What I'm asking is, what are you really here for?*

Writing my mission statement had a much bigger impact than I imagined, and it only took about twenty minutes. I made a long, detailed version because it got the juices flowing, and because I like that sort of thing. But then I made a concise version, and that's the one I revisit. In fact, a sentence or two is best because you can memorize and know it by heart!

Before you think about skipping this exercise because you don't have time ... hold up. You're reading this book because you're ready to do something different, aren't you? And you must trust me at least a smidge, or you wouldn't be here, continuing to turn the pages. So, trust me on this—stop and write the personal mission statement. If you can't do so right this very moment, come back to this as soon as you can. The return on investment (ROI) is *huge*, and it'll keep paying dividends. If nothing else, it'll highlight your roles and the plates you're spinning and may even serve as a wonderful first step in deleting, delegating, deferring, and declining. I'll even walk you through it with examples and templates. You can find these at alessiacitro.com/book.

BE HER NOW EXERCISE:

Make a list of your key values and what you believe your mission is in this lifetime.

BE HER NOW BONUS:

Write a personal mission statement. For inspiration, check out my mission statement at alessiacitro.com/about. There's also a free template waiting for you there.

Chapter 5
Overcoming Limiting Beliefs and Self-Judgment

"There is a vitality, a life force, an energy, a quickening that is translated through you into action, and because there is only one of you in all of time, this expression is unique. And if you block it, it will never exist through any other medium and it will be lost."

—Martha Graham

YOU CONTAIN EVERYTHING YOU NEED

Imagine for a moment, holding an acorn. Within it lies the blueprint and innate intelligence to become a towering oak tree. If conditions are favorable with adequate soil, light, and water, that acorn will indeed grow into an oak tree—maybe one day towering to its full potential at over one hundred feet tall. One day, it will produce acorns, and the cycle will repeat.

Like an acorn, within each of us lies the divine intelligence to grow into something magnificent, to reach heights we can scarcely imagine. Our potential for greatness is innate, simply waiting for us to awaken. My friend … you are anointed. It's all within you *now*, though we tend to forget this truth.

If you planted a seed, would you continuously dig it up to check on its growth because you didn't trust its power to germinate or have roots take hold? Of course, you wouldn't. The same is true for our own growth. We do not need to question our innate potential. Instead, we need to tend the garden that is our mind, body, and spirit.

Stick with me on the plant metaphors for a minute. We sow our potential by planting seeds in our garden. This is focused intention paired with positive emotion, backed by inspired action. And we plant our garden where there is adequate sunlight, because the right environment is life or death.

Then we nourish the seeds and hold our intention through continued action and care. We water our garden and feed the soil. We pull weeds (like negative thoughts and influences) and mitigate pests (naysayers and destructive habits) when they pop up.

If we continue tending our garden, eventually, the seeds we planted will provide beauty and a bountiful, nourishing harvest.

We'll take seeds from the fruits of the harvest and share them with others to plant, and we'll plant some of them too. The harvests will continue as long as we keep tending our garden, sharing the seeds, and sharing our gardening tips … when asked. (Because no one likes unsolicited advice.)

Worth noting that most avid gardeners don't do it for the harvest alone. They garden for the joy of it. Treating our own growth the same way—for the love of the process—is a key to lasting transformation, fulfillment, and happiness. The harvests are a bonus.

A cheesy but effective example. The positive ripple you will create by growing into your Higher Self and sharing those fruits with others is beyond our comprehension. So be her now. Plant and water your seeds.

WIRED TO SURVIVE, NOT THRIVE: THE NEUROSCIENCE OF LIMITING BELIEFS AND SELF-JUDGMENT

The advantage a seed or acorn has that we do not is that it can't think its way out of growing. So long as the conditions are favorable, it *will* grow. Meanwhile, we have the blessing and curse that set us apart from every other species on Earth: the human mind within the prefrontal cortex. This is the seat of our intelligence, and thanks to free will, it can be used for creation or destruction.

Have you ever known someone who had extremely favorable conditions (as far as you know, at least), and yet they failed to realize their potential and "amount to anything," as the saying goes? Or alternatively, maybe you admire someone who completely beat the odds and found success, despite circumstances that would've doomed most to a life of extreme hardship. Herein lies the power of an able human mind. Our minds govern our beliefs, thoughts, emotions, and actions; all of which guide our habits and, thus, our destinies. *We are in control of our minds.* But to wield this power successfully, we must first be empowered with the awareness that we possess it.

Until I learned more about the brain—*why* I had limiting beliefs and *why* I was so self-critical—I was frequently angry with myself. I thought I was defective. I consider myself to be a high-achieving and ambitious person, and it frustrated me to no end that I could not get out of my own way.

This presented in many forms, whether it was giving in to impulses, doing things I knew were dangerous, engaging in self-destructive behaviors, dating people who treated me poorly (including one who became physically abusive), or simply choosing the lower road instead of the higher one. It was subconscious beliefs, programming, comfort, and familiarity that drew me into these scenarios. I'd frequently make the choice that wasn't best for me, and I'd wonder what it was inside me holding this invisible barrier in place, effectively keeping me stuck. The reason is I was addicted to the chemical cocktail the resulting emotions provided. Even if an emotion is what we'd deem negative, like shame or guilt, we are creatures of habit. We are often controlled by our unconscious cravings for a familiar feeling. Even now, with this awareness and understanding, I still battle to break free from these familiar emotions—because they are comfortable.

Can you relate? To continually doing things you *know* are no good for you? To sabotaging yourself and feeling unable to do what you truly want? When I begin working with a client, I frequently hear them confess they are "sick of their own shit." I was too, which is why I wrote this book. If you can't relate, I have wonderful news. You probably don't need this book! For the rest of us, I have good news for you too: *It's not your fault*—it's your brain's ancient design doing its job of keeping you safe by keeping you the same.

Here is where some high-level neuroscience knowledge will set you free from a great deal of self-loathing. There are three layers to the human brain: the reptilian brain, the limbic system, and the neocortex.

The first layer of the brain is the oldest and its characteristics are shared across animal species. This base layer is often referred to as the reptilian brain, and it's about 500 million years old.[14] It gets its name from, you guessed it— reptiles. This layer is tasked with basic survival functions like breathing, heart rate, sex (for the purpose of procreation, not love), and fight-or-flight responses. It's also associated with territorial behavior and the desire for dominance.

Next is the limbic system, the emotional center of the brain. This layer is about 200–300 million years old and came on the scene with mammals. It is responsible for emotions, memory, and motivation.[15] It plays a crucial role in social bonding and processing feelings and experiences. The limbic system also deals with sex, but from the perspective of love and connection. We'll discuss more key structures in the limbic system later, including the amygdala (emotional processing), hippocampus (memory), and hypothalamus (maintaining homeostasis). Of note, the hypothalamus serves as the bridge between the brain's first two layers.

Finally, there's the third layer of the brain—the neocortex. As the name *neo* suggests, this is the newest layer of the brain. It first developed about forty million years ago, with its last major upgrade taking place two to three million years ago. Within the neocortex is the prefrontal cortex. While primates and other species also have prefrontal cortices, ours is more developed and sophisticated, distinguishing us from every other species on Earth.[16] Our sophisticated prefrontal cortex is responsible for higher-order thinking, problem-solving, language, and conscious decision-making. It allows for complex cognitive functions, including reasoning, planning, and creativity.[17] It's a supercomputer between our ears, albeit one that hasn't gotten an upgrade for modern conditions.

LIMITING BELIEFS CAN SERVE A CRITICAL PURPOSE: KEEPING US ALIVE

I believe understanding why we do the things we do and think the thoughts we think is a critical piece in self-mastery. To recognize a limitation and understand it's not us, but a component of our architecture, and then disassociate from it is a very effective way of finding self-compassion *and* solutions. With that, below are eight reasons why we have limiting beliefs, accompanied with modern day examples to help you kick your head trash to the curb.

1. Risk Aversion: Our ancient ancestors who were overly optimistic or took unnecessary risks were less likely to survive. Limiting beliefs can be seen as a form of risk aversion, helping to keep us "safe" in familiar situations. This is a major reason why humans generally resist change.

Modern Day Example: Not buying a home you can afford because you've been conditioned to stash cash for a catastrophe. Or maybe you know someone who was foreclosed on and fear the same fate.

2. Energy Conservation: The brain is an energy hog. It's typically about 2 percent of our body weight and uses 20 percent of our caloric intake.[18] Limiting beliefs can serve to minimize cognitive load, making decision-making more efficient by narrowing down options. (If you've ever experienced decision fatigue at the end of a long day, you know firsthand why our brain was designed to conserve energy where possible.)

Modern Day Example: You have a dream of being an author but keep it shelved because the thought of the process and all that may follow is overwhelming. And I'm not talking about you avoiding the work—I'm talking about the limiting belief of not being good enough, deserving, qualified, etc. Staying in your current lane feels comfortable and removes these unpleasant feelings. (And yes, this was me for years.)

3. Social Cohesion: In early human societies, being part of a group was crucial for survival. If you got kicked out of the tribe, it was like being sent up shit creek without a paddle. Limiting beliefs often align with societal norms and expectations, which can serve to maintain social cohesion.

Modern Day Example: It's Thanksgiving and you're visiting your parents' house. They are very traditional, and you have a new tattoo on your arm they don't know about. They live in a warm climate and there's an unseasonable heat wave. Even though you're uncomfortably hot, you wear long sleeves to avoid them seeing your new ink and judging you. (My younger brother did this to hide his tattoos from our old-school Italian dad for years!)

4. Pattern Recognition: Our brains are inherently designed to recognize patterns to make sense of the world around us. This ability helps us predict and react to situations based on past experiences. However, this process can lead us to perceive patterns where none exist or overgeneralize from a single event. This tendency can give rise to limiting beliefs not supported by evidence or logic.

Modern Day Example: Someone has experienced several failed relationships. They recognize a pattern in these failures and conclude, *all my relationships are doomed to fail.* This belief, although based on a perceived pattern, is an overgeneralization. It doesn't consider the unique circumstances of each relationship or the possibility of change in the future. By assuming that past relationship failures predict future ones, the person may avoid pursuing new relationships or may enter them with a defeatist attitude, thereby contributing to their failure ... and confirming their belief that a pattern existed.

5. Fight, Flight, or Freeze: The amygdala, a key part of the brain involved in processing emotions, plays a significant role in activating the sympathetic nervous system: the fight, flight, or freeze response. This response is a primal mechanism that prepares the body to either confront, flee from, or freeze in the face of perceived threats. Limiting beliefs can be influenced by this system, as the amygdala may trigger emotional responses that lead us to avoid situations perceived as threatening, even if such perceptions are not based on current reality.

Modern Day Example: Public speaking. Often cited as one of the most common fears among people, public speaking surpasses even the fear of death for some. This intense fear can trigger fight, flight, or freeze, even though the situation poses no physical threat. The mere anticipation of standing before an audience can lead an individual to experience a rapid cycle through these responses: feeling an urge to escape the room (flight), becoming combative and defensive in response to anticipated criticism (fight), or standing paralyzed on the stage unable to speak (freeze). If you've ever "pitted out" with stress sweat before a presentation of some kind, you know exactly how this feels.

But *why* do we have these responses? They stem from our deep-seated fear of social rejection or humiliation. As mentioned above with social cohesion, being ostracized from our community meant a decrease in chances of survival, so our brains evolved to treat threats to our social standing as life-threatening. Before a public speaking event, the brain might misinterpret the nervousness and fear of judgment as a signal that our social standing, and therefore our survival, is at risk. This misinterpretation by our well-meaning ancient brain activates the survival response, aiming to protect us from the perceived threat of social banishment.

We can see that an intense reaction to public speaking does not reflect our abilities or the actual danger of the situation but rather an outdated survival mechanism kicking in. Recognizing this can be the first step in managing our fear and approaching many situations with more confidence and less dread.

6. Confirmation Bias: Our brains tend to seek information confirming our existing beliefs and ignore information contradicting them. This is an evolutionary shortcut for quick decision-making but can reinforce limiting beliefs.

Modern Day Example: This book is being published in an American presidential election year, so let's use a timely example of confirmation bias at work. Let's say you strongly support one candidate and vehemently oppose the other. Left unchecked, our wiring toward confirmation bias would lead you to consume media that supports the candidate you like and confirms your loathing of the one you don't. We are naturally wired with the tendency to search for, interpret, favor, and recall information that supports our perspective.

This is why it's so critical to seek out views that differ from your own. Interestingly, the United States Federal Communications Commission (FCC) established a Fairness Doctrine in 1949 that required broadcasters and media outlets to present information in a way that was honest, equitable, and balanced. The policy was eliminated in 1987 for various reasons. Today, most of us live in an echo chamber. All this to say, if you feel very strongly about your viewpoints, have you given them a fair shake? Or have you been reinforcing your views through confirmation bias?

7. **Cognitive Dissonance:** The human brain seeks harmony and consistency among its beliefs, values, and perceptions. Cognitive dissonance occurs when we encounter information or experiences that contrast with our existing beliefs or self-image, leading to psychological discomfort. This discomfort is not merely incidental; it serves an evolutionary purpose by nudging us toward alignment with our social groups' prevailing beliefs and norms. Historically, such alignment was crucial for survival, as being part of a group provided protection, resources, and shared knowledge.

When confronted with evidence that challenges a deeply held limiting belief—perhaps that we cannot achieve success in a certain area of our lives—we experience cognitive dissonance as a form of mental tension. This tension is a signal that our psyche is trying to resolve the inconsistency, either by adjusting our beliefs to accommodate the new information or by dismissing the contradictory evidence to preserve our existing worldview. This mechanism underscores the importance of social cohesion and the lengths to which our minds will go to maintain a sense of internal and social harmony. Recognizing cognitive dissonance in our lives can be a powerful tool for personal growth, prompting us to critically evaluate our beliefs and, where necessary, adopt more empowering and adaptive perspectives.

(Are you beginning to see a theme? We *really* didn't want to get kicked out of the tribe. Is it beginning to make sense why you care so much about what other people think of you, even if you don't like or respect them?)

Modern Day Example: Let's tie this to the previous example of confirmation bias and political media. When presented with evidence contradicting our beliefs about a favored political figure or policy, our natural inclination might be to dismiss or rationalize this information rather than confront the possibility that our initial judgment was flawed. This is akin to playing ostrich and burying our heads in the sand, a defense mechanism that allows us to maintain our existing beliefs without the discomfort of acknowledging contradictory evidence.

Or, when faced with credible reports of our chosen candidate's misconduct, cognitive dissonance may lead us to question the validity of the reports rather than our support for the candidate. Likewise, if we strongly dislike a candidate and come across positive information about their achievements, we might downplay or ignore it to avoid the psychological discomfort of reconciling this new data with our negative perception.

This is why identity politics are such a powerful lever for politicians and pundits. They know how this works, and that you will not vote for a candidate if you believe doing so is at odds with your identity and self-image. Doing so will cause the brain pain of cognitive dissonance!

So, the next time you (or someone you love) dismiss information that contradicts your beliefs, call a timeout and remember that it's our ancient brains at it again.

8. Status Quo Bias: Evolutionarily, maintaining the status quo often meant survival. Limiting beliefs can keep us in our comfort zones, which from an evolutionary standpoint, might have been safer.

Modern Day Example: If you're reading this book, you've lived through major innovations. Novelty is always met with skepticism by some and enthusiasm by others. Like Uber. I'll never forget the first time I got in one. It was 2012 in Chicago. I was out with friends and one ordered an Uber without telling us what he was doing. A black car pulled up to whisk us away as if by magic. I was incredulous! When I shared the experience with friends who lived in places where Uber hadn't become available yet, some of them declared they would never get in a car with a stranger. They'd stick to taxicabs. (Never mind that cab drivers are strangers too.) Fast-forward to today and taxis have largely become relics of the past as the status quo (and our biases) changed.

Rounding out this section on our wiring, it may also be supportive to dig into why you have your specific beliefs. Finding their root can help you dismantle and release them. Otherwise, you'll keep dealing with the smoke instead of the fire. Therapy, hypnotherapy, plant medicine, and journaling are some of the tools that have helped me uproot a lot of my limiting beliefs.

SELF-JUDGMENT HAS ITS BENEFITS

We're all our own worst critics. Like limiting beliefs, the self-judgment mechanism was created to help us survive. Some benefits persist. The key is being fair and objective in our self-awareness to leverage these upsides.

Dopamine is a neurotransmitter in the brain you've probably heard about. It plays a crucial role in our internal reward system, influencing how we experience pleasure, motivation, and satisfaction. It is often released in response to experiences like achieving a goal, receiving positive feedback, or engaging in enjoyable activities. The relationship between dopamine and our experiences is complex, especially when it comes to internal processes like self-judgment.

When we engage in self-judgment, we evaluate our actions, thoughts, or characteristics against our standards or expectations. Positive self-judgment, like acknowledging our achievements or recognizing our strengths, can increase dopamine release. This biochemical response reinforces the behavior or thought pattern being judged positively, contributing to feelings of pleasure, satisfaction, and increased motivation. Completing a challenging task and recognizing your success can trigger a dopamine release, making you feel good and encouraging you to take on similar challenges in the future.

Conversely, negative self-judgment—criticizing ourselves for perceived failures or shortcomings—can affect dopamine levels too. While not directly reducing dopamine release, negative self-judgment can diminish the positive reinforcement typically associated with dopamine. This lack of positive reinforcement can lead to feelings of disappointment, decreased motivation, and sometimes avoidance of activities that might otherwise be rewarding. For example, harshly judging yourself for not meeting a personal goal can dampen the motivation to try again, as the fear of further disappointment overshadows the anticipated reward (and the associated dopamine release). Now you know the neuroscience behind why perfectionism is so poisonous.

Self-judgment isn't all bad, though. There are five notable benefits:

1. Social Cohesion: Self-judgment can serve as a mechanism to ensure that individuals adhere to social norms and expectations, maintaining group cohesion. (Again, we *really* want to stay in the tribe!)

2. Risk Mitigation: Self-judgment can act as an internal check, helping individuals evaluate the risks and rewards of actions. This could be beneficial in avoiding potentially dangerous situations.

3. Resource Allocation: In a group setting, resources are often limited. Self-judgment could regulate one's behavior to ensure a fair distribution of resources, thereby increasing the chances of group survival.

4. Reputation Management: In social species, reputation is important for various forms of cooperation. Self-judgment could help manage one's reputation within a group, which could benefit both the individual and the group.

5. Learning and Adaptation: The discomfort or emotional pain associated with negative self-judgment can serve as a strong motivator for behavioral change, helping individuals adapt to new circumstances or improve skills that are valuable for survival. (I can attest to this as a big driver in why I quit drinking. I was tired of feeling like shit about myself!)

Learning about areas of the brain, their functions, and their potential advantages is exactly how I began to give myself the grace I needed to move forward. If we can stop blaming ourselves and realize these are universal neural architecture obstacles for human beings in the modern world, we will have compassion for ourselves and everyone else we encounter.

BE HER NOW REFLECTION:

Which wiring from our ancient brains do you feel most affected by? Where have these mechanisms been silently running the show without you realizing it? What's an area or situation you can bring more awareness to so that you might evolve your brain to your modern reality?

AN AREA OF THE BRAIN YOU CAN USE TO ACCELERATE YOUR TRANSFORMATION

There's one area of the brain that fascinates me more than any other, and you can use it to your advantage in a big way. It's the reticular activating system (RAS), the brain's information filter. It helps prioritize sensory information, essentially deciding what gets noticed and what gets ignored. It filters out unnecessary information and allows only the most important data to reach higher brain levels for further processing.

The key is, what does your RAS flag as important?

Think of it this way: the RAS functions much like the algorithm on a social media network like TikTok or Instagram, in that it filters out what it thinks you don't care about and only shows you what it thinks you want more of—and deem important. It's why my feed was suddenly full of funny animal videos after I began saving them to show to my daughter.

While the RAS is why you suddenly see that new car you've been thinking about *everywhere*, it also does something else. It filters and prioritizes information based on your thoughts and beliefs, making you more likely to notice and pay attention to what aligns with your current focus. This is the function behind the sayings, "What you focus on, expands" and, "Where attention goes, energy flows." This is why it is absolutely *critical* to focus on positive, healing, and empowering thoughts, as well as the future possibilities you desire.

If you need to breathe belief into yourself, here are some examples of what you can say right now to put your RAS to work *for you*:

"Show me evidence that I am successful."

"Show me evidence that I am capable."

"Show me evidence that I'm farther along than I realize."

"Show me evidence that I have what it takes to realize my dreams."

Your RAS will promptly begin sorting through the vast amount of information it encounters, helping you block out distractions and presenting you with reasons to see your own success, potential, and capability.

Try looking for this affirming evidence and see what happens.

BE HER NOW EXERCISE:

What do you want your RAS to begin serving you evidence of?

We covered a lot in this chapter:

- The infinite intelligence that resides within each of us
- Why our brains keep us in a cycle of judgment and limiting beliefs unless we gain consciousness
- How to utilize your RAS to accelerate your transformation.

BE HER NOW REFLECTION:

Before we move on, reflect on what you've learned in this chapter and what it means for you, specifically. What limiting beliefs and self-judgments can you let go of?

Chapter 6
Reframing Your Internal and External Experience

"To free yourself from the ego's grip, you must see it for what it is: a part of your mind that pretends to be you, but in reality is the source of all inner conflict."

—Eckhart Tolle

GIVE YOURSELF SOME SPACE: DISSOCIATING FROM YOUR INTERNAL HATER

The nagging internal voice that tells me *I can't do* X or *I'm not qualified for* Y feels distinctly *not mine*. Various theories and practices align with and support this.

Buddhist and Taoist philosophies, among others, discuss the concept of *the watcher* or *the observer*, a consciousness separate from the ego and the mind. The idea is to become an observer of your thoughts by detaching from them.

A common analogy for this concept is to liken your thoughts to cars on the road. The idea is to observe the cars passing by; not to run into traffic and get hit.

Creating distance and observing our thoughts doesn't mean the negative voice will get quieter. But it will get easier to stop taking orders from and identifying with it.

So, how can you create distance between yourself and the negative voice? You can label it or personify it. Years ago, I began calling my negative voice "Pam." I created a mental picture of her to further serve as an antidote to the poison of her words. When she gets going, I'll think, *There's Pam, back on her bullshit.* (My apologies to any readers named Pam—I'm sure you're lovely!)

Labeling and personifying the negative voice is great for two reasons. One, it's extremely effective at dissociating from it. By identifying the voice, you can begin to tune it out, ignore it, or override it. Giving your internal chatter another name instantly unlocks observer mode. And it makes it easy to remember it's not you! Two, it brings humor and play. You best believe it brings levity when I think to myself that *Pam is back on her bullshit.*

One more trick that works like magic: When you're speaking negatively of yourself, add *Pam says* before *I am.* Instead of *I am bad with money*, it becomes *Pam says I am bad with money.* How's that for a reframe?

BE HER NOW EXERCISE:

Take a moment now to personify and name your negative voice. The more descriptive, the better. If it feels supportive, journal about this and let it flow. (If you do nothing else, be sure to name your negative voice. Pam comes up a lot throughout the book, and I want you to have *your* voice's name at the ready to sub in.)

SEE THE WORLD AS YOUR MIRROR

"As within, so without; as above, so below."

—Hermes Trismegistus

The law of mirroring and the concept of the social mirror are that every person and interaction serve as a reflection, forcing us to look within. I was introduced to this by the author of this book's foreword, my mentor, Dr. Jenn Chrisman. She shared this concept during my coaching certification, and I felt called out by it. If you do too, it's a natural response. After all, if you've ever done mirror work—the act of looking deeply into your own eyes for reflection, healing, and answers—you know this can be intense and extremely uncomfortable, to a surprising degree.

And so it is in real life. Anything we see in another is a reflection to help us see and experience what we otherwise may not be able to. One way this works is by others reflecting qualities we possess back to us—whether we like them or not. If I feel annoyed or triggered by someone, what about them is causing this reaction in me?

Here's an example of this aspect of the social mirror at work. The Soul Sisters Book Club I facilitate read Debbie Ford's *The Dark Side of the Light Chasers*. In it, she asks the reader to do an exercise: to keep track of everyone who triggers, bothers, or annoys you for one week, to note what was bothersome, and to look for patterns. The purpose? To see the shadow aspects of yourself that you reject, disown, or can't see.

When I did this, the pattern was so obvious I began laughing when I saw it jump off the page of my notebook, as if in flashing lights. Almost every single person who had bothered, triggered, or annoyed me that week had the following qualities in common: incompetent, oblivious, inconsiderate, and loud. What did the woman talking on her cell phone at eighty decibels in a long line at the coffee shop, the man with his shopping cart in the middle of the aisle preventing my passing, and the driver who cut me off all share? The primary characteristics that I disown, dislike, or flat-out reject in myself. In fact, I was sure I didn't have some of these qualities until Debbie lovingly called me out in the pages of her book! If you agree we live in a holographic universe—essentially, that each of us contains every part of the universe—then logic follows we also contain every aspect of human beings within us.

If you reject parts of yourself, people who display those qualities will continue to show up, forcing you to see your shadow in the reflection. You'll get as many opportunities as you need to accept and integrate these parts of yourself to become whole again.

The inverse of this is also true. Imagine for a moment someone you really admire who has a positive effect on you. If you feel starstruck or in awe of someone, they are providing a mirror, reflecting wonderful parts of you that you haven't fully claimed or stepped into yet. If you didn't possess the qualities that you admire in them, how would you be able to recognize these attributes? Perhaps these gifts are latent, waiting for you to remember your potential and awaken to the force within you! When someone affects you like this, Debbie calls it your *light shadow*. I invite you to see which qualities are present in those you admire and to begin letting your own light shine. You might be a lighthouse for someone else to step into and claim their light shadow!

Here's another way the social mirror works: It'll serve up *experiences* that provide opportunities to be the person you say you are or want to be. This is why I don't believe in true coincidence. Maybe it's delusional or "delulu," but I really do believe that everything happens *for* me and for the greater good—even when it's uncomfortable, unpleasant, or downright heartbreaking.

The following is not a story I planned to share, but I can think of no better example to illustrate this concept, so here it goes.

While attending a program to earn my coaching certification, an unlikely "coincidence" forced me to see a painful reflection and pattern. It was the end of the first day, and we'd learned and used a potent modality to release anger. Much of the anger and rage I'd been suppressing was around people-pleasing and deep shame—specifically with men I'd been intimately involved with. A mental slideshow of every man (and sometimes his mother) who'd made me feel ashamed in some way began to roll in my mind like a film reel. It was emotionally exhausting, and the day concluded with puffy eyes and smeared mascara.

I began retreating to my room, hoping to avoid any and all human interaction. And then, as if on cue, I heard a man call my name. I turned to look and saw Paul. (Not his real name.)

Paul and I had a lengthy history going back to freshman year of college. The CliffsNotes version of our story is that we liked each other, fooled around, and years later became "friends with benefits" when we lived in the same city after graduation. We were never in a committed relationship, even though I would've been willing. (What's that saying about buying a cow when you're getting free milk?) With Paul, it was common for me to be eager and available in an effort to please him and tip the scales. (Luckily, I learned this doesn't work *before* I met Jeff!)

This run-in was highly improbable. Paul lived across the country from this hotel. This wasn't like running into your neighbor at the grocery store.

When I saw Paul, it was as if a physical representation of my people-pleasing tendencies manifested in front of me to face and release. Paul was *exactly* who I needed to run into that day, though I didn't realize it in the moment.

I don't remember the substance of our conversation, but before parting ways he suggested we go on a walk the next morning. When this happened, I'd been happily married for years, and he, too, was in a serious relationship. While I don't doubt it was an innocent invitation or some pleasantry word vomit, it forced me to pause and consciously *decide* who I wanted to be. (Sure, a walk seems benign, but would you want your partner going for a stroll with an old flame? I know I wouldn't!)

The next morning, I'm not proud to admit I briefly considered texting him. Not because I actually gave a damn about going on a walk with him, but because my pattern of people-pleasing—and my pattern of doing so *with him*—was so ingrained. A natural reflex, like some habits can become. Luckily, consciousness came in, as if awaking while sleepwalking. I felt a surge of clarity and didn't text him. My Higher Self prevailed, and I went for a walk alone.

Once I confronted this pattern, which was served up on a silver platter that day, it lost its power over me. People-pleasing isn't something I struggle with anymore. And I've never heard from or seen Paul again.

Sometimes it happens in odd ways, like this run-in did, but the universe always supports our growth and has our back. Of all the days this could have happened, it was the same day

I released shame and anger around this specific pattern. It was the same day I showed up to do the work so I could coach others through similar experiences. And it was *the same day* I first learned the concept of the social mirror from Dr. Jenn and why these "coincidences" happen at all! It was divinely orchestrated, and you can't convince me otherwise.

No two experiences will look the same; this is how the experiential mirror works. These opportunities, which often present as, and feel like, tests, will continue and escalate until we receive the message. If you're receptive and recognize what's being offered, you may make a decision that affirms the life and identity you desire. This type of opportunity might feel gentle, like a feather.

On the other hand, if you're closed off or stubborn, these learning opportunities will likely continue until you learn through what feels like a sledgehammer. I've learned lessons both ways, and the feather is greatly preferred.

Before we move on, take a moment here to think about some of the unlikely encounters you've had. Maybe with a stranger who changed the trajectory of your life, or perhaps with someone who brought with them a blast from the past and an opportunity to heal it. In retrospect, what happened (or not) because of that run-in? Let me give you some personal examples to get your memory juices flowing.

- Todd, a gentleman I waited on while working in a Chicago bar who ended up giving me a job at his public relations firm. Of note, I only had his table because my friend begged to be "cut" so she could study for an exam. This job provided essentials skills I continue to use as an entrepreneur.

- Lisa, the recruiter who found me on Monster.com (I know, I'm really dating myself) who helped me land a job at lightning speed in 2009 when no one was hiring ... and reached out because we'd been in the same sorority. My boss at that job, Norma, was like a second mother to me while I lived far from home and navigated the shitstorm of my early twenties. She prepped me well for the rest of my career, and we're still close today.

- Jodie, the woman I met on a plane who was my sign to leave my job at Google. We weren't supposed to be seated together, but Jeff and I got upgraded and split up. Jodie continues to be a guiding light, business mentor, and force for good in my life.

- The (almost) business partner who tried to extort me after we parted ways. She taught me many valuable lessons with a feather. Lessons that would've felt like a sledgehammer if I'd learned them later. She also introduced me to one of my closest friends whom I'll be forever grateful for, and who has connected me to countless others who have been instrumental on my path.

- The internet troll whose comment helped me realize I had released (at least some of) my fear around public criticism and being personally attacked online. I've since been able to show up bigger, bolder, and unapologetically.

If no personal experiences come to mind right now, that's okay. Let this marinate. Think about pivotal moments in your life, important people who have shaped you (for better or worse), and then connect the dots backward. See how many opportunities you've been given to take the path you desire and be the person you know you can be.

BE HER NOW EXERCISE:

Most people go through life unconsciously, in a walking coma of sorts, and they never realize they're looking at a reflection. We all do this to an extent, but I encourage you to bring conscious intention to experiencing the mirror. What about yourself have you been rejecting or disowning? What admirable qualities have you been sleeping on? What experiences keep happening, beckoning you to affirm the identity and reality you desire? Journal or meditate on this if it feels supportive.

Now that we've laid the groundwork for overcoming negativity inside and out, the next chapter is all about facing your fears. Let's go.

Chapter 7

Common Fears and How to Move Past Them

"Don't wait until you're 'perfect' or 'qualified' to go after what you want. You're already enough, and you'll figure it out along the way."

—Marie Forleo

COURAGE

At time of writing, my daughter is five years old. A repeated point of contention at home was that she refused to go to the bathroom by herself. Not because she couldn't or needed my help, but because she felt scared. At first, this frustrated me. I want to foster independence in her, and the bathroom is *right there!*

Initially, I thought it was a ploy for attention. It soon became clear that her fear was very real. With curiosity, I finally asked her why she felt afraid. Her reply was that she felt scared because of "zombies and monsters" in the hallway. I reassured her that monsters and zombies aren't real, and if they are, we definitely don't have any in our house. But she didn't buy it. And to the bathroom with her I went.

As I got into bed that night, a light bulb lit up in my mind. I fear plenty of shit that's not real: failure and judgment, thousands of "what-ifs," ego tantrums, etc. Why do I experience frustration or surprise that she feels afraid of stuff that doesn't exist? She's five years old—what's my excuse?

With legitimately dangerous situations and those requiring vigilance being exceptions, fear is usually a liar. A helpful acronym for FEAR is *False Evidence Appearing Real*. Like the purpose of limiting beliefs, our lizard brain wants to do its job and keep us safe. As discussed in Chapter 5, it can equate the nerves of public speaking with a bear chasing us. How can we recognize our nervous system's response, thank our brain for doing its job and working to protect us, and then begin to release the fear?

To do so, here is an antidote for when our ancient survival mechanisms kick in and aren't needed. While there are many ways to ground back into safety when we feel triggered and our sympathetic ("fight-or-flight") nervous system activates, the below is one of my favorites—a synthesis of various tools.

First, I bring awareness to the fear and the response I'm having. I acknowledge it and shift my awareness to feeling the support of the ground or the furniture below. I breathe deeply, usually in a box format (breathe in for four counts, hold for four, exhale for four, hold for four). This helps to lower heart rate and calm both body and mind. I will say out loud or silently, *I am safe.*

If I'm especially triggered and fearful, I'll imagine myself as a kid or the past version of me that's causing me to experience the emotional response. I'll visualize giving these parts of me a tour of my present life and reality. For example, money and fear of scarcity are regular triggers and fears that pop up for me. When this happens, I give a *Lifestyles of the Rich & Famous* meets MTV *Cribs* style tour of my current life to these affected past versions. In this case, little girl Alessia and broke twenty-something me. I show them my beautiful home, car, loving husband, bank account balances, and how well-resourced *we* are now. I realize this may sound bizarre, but it's been one of the most effective tools in my belt. It's also a very effective means of getting into a state of gratitude. If you can, think of a common fear or trigger you experience, and then note how different things are now than when this fear was seeded.

When I'm ready to return to my body, I'll place my hands in front of my eyes, slowly open them, and ground back into my body and surroundings. I'll note the colors in the room and feel the texture of my clothing, the furniture, or the floor under my bare feet. I'll take a sip of water if it's available. I'll touch my face and tap my arms and legs. After doing this exercise, the fear may still be present. But it's no longer in control.

When it comes to fear, perhaps we need to adjust our expectations. For a long time, I kept waiting for fear to go away. Finally, I realized it never does. It just loses its grip. John Wayne once said, "Courage is being scared to death, but saddling up anyway." I know, The Duke is an unlikely source to quote, but he was spot on. Courage is not the absence of fear. It's feeling scared, using available tools to diminish it (if possible), coping, and forging ahead.

It's easy to look at people ahead of us, especially in entrepreneurship, and think these folks are superhuman and don't experience fear. Turns out, they do too. I've been to enough events and conferences to hear many of my personal heroes say so onstage. They readily admit they feel scared all the time and that it doesn't get easier. They just get stronger and better at acting, despite their fear, *courageously*.

When you act when you're scared shitless, it could be you're an adrenaline junkie. More likely, it's because *the upside is bigger than your fear.* That is the only reason you're reading this book. To write it, I acted despite my stomach turning from fear because I knew you needed to read this, right here and now. And you may be here staring your own fear in the face, courageously preparing to get out of your own way ... for good.

Fear had me in a mental ditch, and I can pinpoint the day I was pulled out. I launched my first ground-up business in early 2022 and, shortly thereafter, shuttered it. I spent fifteen months licking my wounds, coming up with a myriad of reasons why I wasn't knowledgeable enough or good enough to start again. Luckily, I continued to surround myself with high vibe, visionary leaders who were *doing the damn thing,* and I kept putting myself in rooms with them. If you don't believe in yourself right now, here's a nudge to borrow the belief of others. See your light shadow in them and your story in theirs. They'll start to rub off on you.

Case in point: when magic struck at the incredible Powerhouse Women event hosted by Lindsey Schwartz. The message I repeatedly heard from every speaker that day was to take action, *now.* They were speaking right to me, beckoning me to look fear in the face and *be her now!* Then came the moment I was pulled from the ditch. Dr. Emily Jacobs took the stage. She shared that her young daughters were in the back of the room watching her. I turned and saw them standing there, beaming with such pride for their mother. I felt a shift and click. *I will do this for my daughter! If I am to help her confidently and courageously pursue her own vision one day, I must go first! I must walk the walk! I will do this for all those who have come before me and who will come after!*

The inner dialogue really was that dramatic. Pam must've taken the day off because I didn't hear her once. Since that day, I've been in persistent momentum, knowing the reasons to keep forging ahead are how I can, will, and must serve others. To continue leading from the front. How can we expect to lead others if we can't first lead ourselves?

So, let me ask you a critical question that demands an answer. **What is your** *why*? If you haven't yet, this is your invitation to *find your why with eyes*. It changes everything.

Here's a tried-and-true way to uncover your real *why*. Write down what you think your *why* is, and for each answer, ask yourself, Why? again. Peel back the layers of this onion until you get to *the why that makes you cry*, or the why that resonates deep within you as your *real* driver.

To go deep on your *why*, here are some questions to consider.

- Why does your vision for your life deeply matter to you?
- Who will you be serving by working toward your vision and fulfilling it?
- Who is waiting for your message, the way only you can deliver it?
- Who were you created to be?

If a dream is in your heart, it was put there for a reason.

Here's what this looks like in practice. Let's say your surface level *why* is to make more money. Okay, *why* is that important? Perhaps it's so you can stop living paycheck to paycheck. Well, *why* is that important? Maybe financial stress is causing you to lash out at your family or it's deteriorating your health. And *why* does that matter? Could be that you don't want to repeat a dysfunctional pattern or don't want to die of a heart attack prematurely like someone you know did … And you keep going on and on asking *why* until you hit gold. When I created this exercise for a large team I was leading, I first did it myself, and I realized my *why* was rooted in fear. I felt (and still feel!) afraid of being broke and all the obstacles that come with it.

But don't stop at fear. If you do, you'll operate from that place. And fear can be a liar, remember? Instead, how can you transmute a motivation rooted in fear to one that is rooted in love? Love is our true essence. A motivation rooted in love guides you like a North Star, keeping you in alignment with your purpose and mission. It'll also be far more powerful, meaningful, and long-lasting. If you're running from fear, it's exhausting and unfulfilling. Instead, run toward love, service, and what lights you up.

When you feel fear pop up again (and it will), consider this powerful insight from Marianne Williamson's A *Return to Love*: "The presence of fear is a sure sign we're trusting in our own strength." When you feel afraid, can you open to receiving help, whether it's from friends, family, loved ones, or a Higher Power? Remember: Ask, and it is given. Open your heart. You don't need to go it alone.

Speaking of heart, look at the word *courage*. It's derived from the Latin word *cor*, meaning *heart*. Remember your why, rooted in love, and watch fear lose its grip on you.

A final note on fear and other constrictive emotions that can keep us from becoming our Higher Selves. Like we dissociate from our negative voice (*Hi, Pam!*), you can also create distance from your emotions. I don't personify my emotions with names and traits (although you certainly can if you'd like to), but I consciously try to stop identifying *as* them. When I think something like, *I'm mad right now*, I try to catch myself. No, I *am not* mad. I *feel* mad. We are not our anger, our sadness, our shame. We *feel* these! They are transitory; not identifying, permanent characteristics. Unless of course, we allow them to be. "I am"—the two most powerful words in the universe. Utter them with reverence and intention.

Some research indicates that when an emotion is triggered, the chemical of the feeling is flushed through the bloodstream and fully absorbed by the body in less than ninety seconds.[19] (Of course, our thoughts about it may prolong the emotional experience.) Our identity is what persists, not our emotional states of being. So, let's take steps to stop identifying as our emotions. Deal?

OVERCOMING YOUR PAST

So many of us are being held back by past versions of us, as if they were ghosts. They no longer exist, but they haunt us all the same.

Remember in the opening chapter when I told you I sold wine online? Well, I started that business shortly before the COVID-19 pandemic hit. As you'd expect, my business experienced explosive growth as people were stuck at home, wanted to drink, and looked for extra income in a time of great uncertainty. Selling wine in the volume I was, I earned cases upon cases of free or deeply discounted wine. This was an incentive intended to cut the costs of hosting wine tastings to grow the business. But during the pandemic (in California, no less), social gatherings weren't happening. Stuck at home for months with boxes of wine showing up weekly was the perfect storm. In less than a year, I became a high-functioning alcoholic. Looking back, I'd always had questionable drinking behavior, but the pandemic took it to new heights.

I used alcohol to numb out and escape multiple parts of my reality that troubled me: being "quarantined" in our home, the fear of my family or me getting sick or dying, my tech sales career circling the drain, and the stress of parenting a toddler (while working) without available childcare, to name a few. This may have been *normal* behavior in 2020, but it was far from *optimal*. I brought so many people into the wine business who also developed problematic drinking behavior, many of whom were women and moms with young kids. It's something that has deeply haunted me. But I also believe, as my friend Sandy says, that "Your mess becomes your message."

I stopped drinking alcohol on June 13, 2022. It felt like a rebirth, and my life improved in every area. I began to experiment with moderation in January 2023, quickly remembered I can't moderate *anything*, and went alcohol-free for good on April 1, 2023. I opened up about my journey early on and, by doing so, have helped many others stop drinking. Getting sober is also what catalyzed my path in habits. Would I have been able to do any of this if I hadn't ventured far enough into alcohol use disorder myself? No!

There are plenty of other periods of my personal history I'm not proud of. Being mean and judgmental. Stirring the pot. Peer-pressuring people to do things that weren't always positive. Devaluing myself with men. And plenty, plenty more. You might have a long list too. But if we let these past ways of being keep us from evolving and stepping into our higher calling, we're missing the point of being alive.

As an imperfect human, I take great comfort in a concept discussed in Neale Donald Walsch's extraordinary book *Conversations with God*. Sometimes, we must experience Who We Are Not to remember Who We Are. Sometimes, being the opposite of Who We Are is exactly what's needed to awaken, appreciate, and step into our true nature. If we can transmute our past to become teachers and healers, we shouldn't be so hard on ourselves.

Don't be afraid to pivot and change, even if it looks like an overhaul of your former self. Evolution toward your truth is what you're here for.

YOU ARE NOT AN IMPOSTOR

The term "Impostor Syndrome" was first coined by psychologists Pauline Rose Clance and Suzanne Ament Imes in a 1978 paper titled *The Impostor Phenomenon in High Achieving Women: Dynamics and Therapeutic Intervention.*[20] The study initially focused on high-achieving women who felt they did not deserve their accomplishments and lived in fear of being exposed as "frauds."

Impostor Syndrome is characterized by feelings of inadequacy, self-doubt, and a fear of being exposed as fraudulent despite evidence of competence and expertise. This is exactly how I felt before I began writing this book. *Who was I to write a book on habits?* Well, aside from the go-to experts, I'm unaware of anyone who knows as much about habits as I do, or who's learned as many hard lessons in how important they are. Who am I *not* to write this book?

What's *your* version of this?

It's like we expect someone to come anoint us and say, "Okay, you're qualified and ready now!" How many times have you (or your version of Pam) told yourself something like the following? *Who am I to write a book? I don't have a degree in behavioral science or a certification in this area. I know I've read a lot of books on the subject, and I've had my own transformation, but I don't have enough knowledge or experience to help others or teach on this.*

This was the exact talk track Pam wouldn't stop spouting. And I believed it for a while. It wasn't until I began outlining this book that I realized how much I knew. Then it was like a dam breaking, and I wished I hadn't waited so long. More experiential tax I've paid to hopefully spare you from doing the same thing!

Let me ask you the same question from above, in a different way. What are you well-equipped to take action on *right now*?

Seriously. Stop for a moment and ask yourself: *What are you disqualifying yourself from?*

You are ready. You'll figure the rest out as you go. You were born for such a time as this.

Remember when we talked about men applying for a job when they're 60 percent qualified and women waiting until they've met 100 percent of the qualifications? Yeah, we aren't doing that anymore. You know enough right now to start pursuing your dream! I have heard it that if you know 10 percent more than the person you're trying to teach, or if you're one to two steps ahead of them, you know enough to start helping. And dare I say, there is a great deal of value provided by those who are still actively in the trenches compared to someone who is way farther along. Sometimes, those who are in the thick of it are precisely those we learn the most from.

PLAYERS GONNA PLAY AND HATERS GONNA HATE

"It is not the critic who counts; not the man who points out how the strong man stumbles, or where the doer of deeds could have done them better. The credit belongs to the man who is actually in the arena, whose face is marred by dust and sweat and blood; who strives valiantly; who errs, who comes short again and again, because there is no effort without error and shortcoming; but who does actually strive to do the deeds; who knows great enthusiasms, the great devotions; who spends himself in a worthy cause; who at the best knows in the end the triumph of high achievement, and who at the worst, if he fails, at least fails while daring greatly, so that his place shall never be with those cold and timid souls who neither know victory nor defeat."

—Theodore Roosevelt

My first success in business outside of the corporate tech setting was in network marketing. I knew I had the right opportunity at the right time. Having failed at network marketing before, I was done playing small and fearing what people might think. (To hell with that pesky wiring toward social cohesion, am I right?) Nevertheless, I was stuck on how to overcome this until I turned on Netflix one night in 2019. It suggested a new special for me: *Brené Brown: The Call to Courage*. As I watched intently, she shared the aforementioned Teddy Roosevelt quote.

It was like a lightning bolt hit me.

Why was I so worried about the peanut gallery? I was letting the potential opinions of other people hold me back from going for something I really wanted. Despite my fear, I vowed to go for it. I took courageous first steps in sharing the opportunity and immediately felt liberated. That quote was what got me over the hump. In two years, I built a team of almost 1,000 people that brought in nearly $3 million in total revenue. It's incredible what shedding the weight of other people's potential opinions can do.

Remember in Chapter 5 when we talked about how our brains work to keep us from getting kicked out of the tribe? Well, this wiring came in handy when that was how we lived. Getting kicked out of the tribe and into the wilderness was tantamount to a death sentence. And so, our brains tell us to acquiesce and not make waves—whether it's with your relatives at dinner or the acquaintance from your small-town high school who still follows you on Instagram. If you pursue your full expression, sure, maybe some naysayers will come out of the woodwork. But is appeasing these hypothetical haters more important than realizing your potential and serving the people who need you, who may not even know you yet?

If and when you do get negative comments, either in real life or on the internet, know it's not about you, it's about them. As we discussed in the last chapter, triggers happen because they're a mirror, showing us the qualities we have and disown, or the experiences we desire but haven't attained or had the courage to go for yet. If you're triggering someone, you're merely inviting them to use the magic of the social mirror.

A final thought here: You will never be criticized by someone more successful than you. They might not agree with your marketing strategy or might see gaps you can't, but they won't hate on you for trying or use condescension. The only people who will are the people who want you to do less so they can feel better about staying the same ... and stuck. Bless and release them, and go play your game.

BE HER NOW REFLECTION:

Whose opinion is holding you back? Who's sitting in the nosebleeds, affecting your performance in the arena (or keeping you out of it altogether)?

BABY, DON'T WORRY ABOUT A THING

We waste so much time and energy worrying about things that never happen. I have the data to prove it. One study found that 91.39 percent of all worries did not materialize in reality.[21] Another found that when worries did manifest, nearly 80 percent of participants found their challenges were either more manageable than they had anticipated or provided valuable life lessons.[22]

What's the worst that could happen if you go for it? Seriously. Catastrophize if you need to and if it feels supportive. Going to a worst-case scenario is sometimes exactly how to realize it wouldn't be so bad, and that we could handle it or figure it out. While you're at it, keep things balanced and go to the best-case scenario too.

If you're a natural worrier, I know this is easier said than done. It's been said that depression is worrying about the past while anxiety is worrying about the future. Many of us (including me) indulge in or suffer from both. When I find myself in either state, I follow the stages of the *Higher Self Habits* method outlined in this book, which can be applied to any scenario. It only takes a moment to run through:

1. Become *aware* of where you're placing your focus.
2. *Align* with the person you want to be and consider what they would think, feel, and do about the situation you're fretting over.
3. *Audit* what you can control and what you need to let go of. (Bless and release!)
4. Once you have an action step, *activate* and do what's necessary.
5. And finally, celebrate yourself and *ascend* into a better headspace.

Let's be clear—anxiety and depression are more than just worrying, and I say this as someone actively on antidepressants with a prescription for anxiety meds to take when needed. If you also suffer from anxiety, depression, or both, please don't misinterpret what I'm saying as advice to suppress, think, and do your way out of it. And yet, when the going gets tough, what *can* you do to help yourself when it comes to your thoughts, actions, and who you're choosing to embody? I know those of us with depression and anxiety walk a line here, and I believe it's important to help ourselves in every way possible.

Here's the other thing about worrying. It's always because of uncertainty. How can we become more comfortable with uncertainty? Is it a matter of adding novelty into your day? Brushing your teeth with the opposite hand and taking a different route on your commute are benign ways to do this. (Don't knock it until you've tried it.)

You may also need to change or let go of expectations. It may be worth evaluating how much of your worrying is rooted in perfectionism or control. Could you begin to surrender a bit more? Or become more open to the timeline for your desires to transpire? Or perhaps you need to relinquish your attachment to the packaging your desires show up in? Doing this changes your energy to feel lighter. It creates spaciousness for joy and miracles to enter. Try it and see. Unclench, holding your why and your vision in the forefront of your mind, and let go— especially of the how, what, and when.

BE HER NOW REFLECTION:

What worries are outside of your control that you can let go of, knowing you will be able to handle them on the off chance they come to pass?

Now that you're aware of many ways we are wired to play and stay small, let's align to our Higher Selves.

Part Two: Align

"Alignment is not about arranging circumstances in your favor, but about aligning your own heart and mind with the flow of life. When you are in alignment, life unfolds with a natural rhythm that guides your steps and fills your journey with purpose."

—Unknown

Chapter 8

Expand Your Perception to Expand Your Legacy

"What you do makes a difference, and you have to decide what kind of difference you want to make."

—Jane Goodall

STEPPING OUT OF THE FRAME TO SEE THE [BIG] PICTURE

In May 2022, I was asked to write and deliver my beloved grandparents' eulogy at their joint memorial service. For a week I wrote, refined, and rewrote. The tears flowed. I had been tasked with doing justice to a collective 195 years of well-lived life. It forced me to consider what would be said at my own funeral versus what I would *want* to be said, and to reflect on my own legacy and where I was headed. This introspection on my priorities and values was like warning sirens going off. I was focused on earning accolades and making money more than I was on my beautiful young family, my health, and my mission of service. I was indeed going the wrong way, and it was time to course correct.

An Oliver Wendell Holmes quote comes to mind here: "Alas for those that never sing, but die with all their music in them!"

How would you feel if you received a terminal diagnosis tomorrow, knowing you didn't answer your soul's calling and never went after your dreams? If you spent your life chasing after the wrong shit or didn't share your gifts with the world?

To leave the Earth without fulfilling your calling or expressing your unique genius is tragic. At the time of this writing, the world population has passed eight billion. Imagine all the people who have come before you and who will come after. And YOU will never exist (in this unique form and incarnation) again.

So, what have you been uniquely endowed with? What talents, genius, and gifts are you sleeping on and withholding? We need them, my friend!

The reasons for holding back are nearly universal. It can feel scary to show up authentically—to create something and put it out there. It's why I'm writing this book at the age of thirty-eight when I've wanted to be an author since my earliest memories. And yes, I will come back and reference this section when someone inevitably leaves a bad review about this book. No doubt, bad reviews will sting and may hurt my feelings. But it hurts more to think about the people I wouldn't impact and to die with the dream in me. Do you agree? If so, what have you been holding back?

BE HER NOW EXERCISE:

Imagine writing your obituary or eulogy at the end of a very long, healthy, intentional, and fulfilling life of impact. What would your life have been like? Where do you see gaps between your current trajectory and where you want to end up?

OPENING UP TO POSSIBILITIES

It's time to begin stepping into your gifts, potential, and light. We are about to vision cast together, but first, I invite you to revisit the limiting beliefs and self-judgments we dispelled in Chapters 5 and 6. When you catch your version of Pam spewing negative and doubtful chatter, observe that inner dialogue and ask yourself: *What else could be true?*

For example, if you catch yourself thinking you're not a good enough writer to publish a book, stop and ask: *What else could be true?* Perhaps you have incredible verbal communication. You could dictate your book—who says you must type it? Or maybe you never did well on spelling tests and have terrible grammar and punctuation. *What else could be true?* You have a computer—and it has an internet connection that enables you to spell-check and use Grammarly. Whatever the limiting belief and perceived problem, there is always a solution if we're willing to seek it.

If you scoffed at that last statement, ask yourself honestly: Are you fighting more for your limitations or your possibilities?

Possibilities carry responsibility. We all talk about fearing failure, but many of us fear success just as much or more. But you must draw your line in the sand. Your Higher Self has unsung music to belt out. Like she's in the shower, covering Celine Dion's greatest hits. (If you know, you know.)

One of the most important steps we can take toward possibility is to step into *the identity of a victor*, not a victim. Taking radical responsibility for everything in your life can be brutal, depending on the state of things, but it is the most empowering thing you can do. There may be systems stacked against you, a complete and utter lack of support and resources, or a deficit you're working out of. But if you decide that you are the one who can change your circumstances come hell or high water, isn't that a much more empowered position than believing you're at the mercy of external forces? A belief in victory attracts the solution. (More on that in the next chapter.)

Those with much to overcome often end up being some of the most successful among us. They understand how fortunate they are because of the polarity and wide frame of reference they've personally experienced. If talent, resources, or favorable conditions come easy, we sometimes don't value them as much and don't feel the same level of motivation to maximize and perpetuate their utility.

One example is the widely cited statistic that 90 percent of generational wealth is lost by the third generation that inherits it. No doubt, one reason is that third-generation heirs may take the money for granted because they don't know any different. They weren't alive to witness the victor mentality and action it took to create the wealth, and thus, they may not have the character and experience to maintain it. This is a great illustration of *easy come, easy go*. There's something to be said for sustained work over time. The acquisition process often provides a blessing in disguise, whether that be greater appreciation, stewardship, or the knowing you can make it happen. That work of building can have enjoyment and ease—it doesn't need to feel like a struggle.

Whatever is going on in your life right now—know that you have the capacity, the talent, the gifts, and the life force to transmute and alchemize your circumstances into gold. What if the circumstances you're up against now are teaching you the grit and skills to provide a bigger blessing down the road? A mantra I say often is, "Everything is always working out for me." Even if it can seem like a cruel cosmic joke that we can't understand, believe that it's true. What if everything happens *for* you?

EXPAND YOUR PERCEPTION TO UNLOCK YOUR POTENTIAL

If you're ever doubting your place in the world, pause and consider the incredible fact that we, our planet, and the entire universe are even here. As a matter of fact, for the universe to exist as it is, the balance between electromagnetism and gravity needs to be exact—with electromagnetism around $10^{\wedge}36$, or 10 to the 36th power stronger than gravity.[23] (Yes, that's 1 with 36 zeros, or a trillion trillion trillion.) If this delicate balance shifted ever so slightly—like adding or removing a single grain of sand from a scale that's perfectly balancing a car—the existence of stars, planets, and life as we know it would be impossible. With more than two hundred such critical conditions in the universe, even the smallest change could have prevented it from being here.[24] And yet, here we are.

Do you really think our cosmic reality came to life in perfect orchestration, but somehow, this same infinite intelligence created YOU with defects? Not a chance. Despite what Pam or your discouraging voice within might argue, remember this when doubt ensnares you. We are simultaneously a minuscule fragment of the vast finely-tuned universe and an essential piece of its intricate puzzle.

The next time that negative voice becomes convincing, ask again: *What else can be true?* Sometimes a different perspective is all that's needed.

In the beginning of Stephen Covey's classic, *The 7 Habits of Highly Effective People*,[25] is an image that can be seen in two different ways. Depending on how the viewer is primed, they will see it the way they were told to. Covey shares an experiment where students were split into two groups. One group was primed to see the image one way; the other group, the opposite way. After separately viewing the image, they came back together and were incredulous that they didn't see the same thing. They argued about it and were convinced the other group was wrong. Eventually, they came to understand how they were able to see different pictures within the same image. Applying this to how you see yourself, is it possible that perhaps you view yourself in a critical way, at least in part because of programming and outside influences that led you to accept it as truth? Is it possible that you could see yourself in another, positive way, if only you were primed to do so? (Which is what I'm attempting to do here, in case you were wondering.)

The image Covey shares in his book is below in Figure 8.1.[26] Do you see an old woman or a young woman? Can you see both? If so, does this serve as a visual reminder of how two perspectives can exist simultaneously? If not, is it possible you still have work to do in expanding your ability to see outside of your own perception?

Figure 8.1: "My Wife and My Mother-In-Law" by William Ely Hill. Do you see the pretty young woman? Or the elderly mother-in-law?

If you see yourself in a way that is not supportive of your dreams and your potential, I invite you to shift your perspective and paradigm. See yourself in the way that those who love and admire you, your creator, and your Higher Self do.

BUILD THE BRIDGE OF SELF-BELIEF

You're reading this because you know and believe on some level you can become a better version of yourself. Sometimes you may feel more negatively about yourself than you do optimistic. You've likely heard of the power of affirmations, and perhaps you or those you know have discounted them as being "woo-woo," or fluffy at best. Affirmations can build the bridge of self-belief and here's how, from a neuroscientific perspective:

- **Neuroplasticity:**[27] Affirmations can influence neuroplasticity, which is the brain's ability to reorganize and adapt by forming new neural connections. When you repeat positive affirmations, you engage certain neural pathways associated with those thoughts. Over time, this repetition can strengthen those pathways, making the positive beliefs more automatic.

- **Positive Reinforcement:**[28] Affirmations can trigger the brain's reward system. When you use positive affirmations, it can stimulate the release of dopamine, a neurotransmitter associated with pleasure and reward. This can create a positive association with the affirmation, reinforcing the belief.

- **Reduction of Negative Self-Talk:**[29] The brain tends to latch onto negative thoughts, leading to self-doubt and low self-esteem. Affirmations disrupt this cycle by replacing negative thoughts with positive ones.

- **Self-fulfilling Prophecy**:[30] Believing the affirmations you repeat can lead to a self-fulfilling prophecy. When you truly believe in your abilities and potential, you are more likely to take action and make choices aligned with those beliefs, increasing the chances of success. (This is also because you've shifted your identity. More on that soon.)

- **Subconscious Programming**:[31] The subconscious mind tends to respond better to present-tense statements. It processes information in a more literal and immediate way, so framing affirmations as if they're already true has a more profound impact on subconscious beliefs and behaviors. (If you've ever made a vision board from a first-person perspective, as in, choosing images from the perspective from which you'd experience them, this is the same concept.)

- **Placebo Effect**:[32] While not directly related to neuroscience, the placebo effect is a psychological phenomenon that demonstrates the power of belief. If you believe affirmations will work, you may experience positive changes simply because you expect to.

Let's go a bit deeper on this last point to illustrate how powerful our minds are. If you're not familiar with the concept of a placebo, it's a substance or treatment with no active therapeutic effect, like a sugar pill. Placebos are often used in clinical trials as a control to test the efficacy of new medications. In trials, participants are given either the placebo or the actual drug, and neither the participants nor the researchers know who receives which. This helps to eliminate bias and determine if the drug works better than not receiving any treatment at all.

For example, a sugar pill might be used as a placebo when testing a new medication for headaches. If the patients taking the sugar pill report relief from their headaches, it's considered a placebo effect. This effect is powerful because it demonstrates that our expectations and beliefs can influence our physical health, even when the treatment itself isn't directly addressing the medical issue.

Here's where this gets interesting and how it can help you change your life. A *placebo can work even when you know you are taking a placebo.* In one randomized study,[33] forty patients with irritable bowel syndrome (IBS) were given a bottle with a clear label: *Placebo Pills.* They were told the pills were "made of an inert substance, like sugar pills, that have been shown in clinical studies to produce significant improvements in IBS symptoms through mind-body, self-healing processes." There was a second group of forty patients given no pills that served as a control group. Sure enough, the patients who took the placebos had twice as much relief from symptoms as the control group. They *knew* they were taking a placebo, but because they were primed to believe these pills worked, they did! The "mind-body, self-healing processes" really did work.

Just like how a sugar pill can be as effective as actual medication (if a person believes the placebo is the real thing or will work), you can likewise "trick" your mind into believing positive statements—*if you believe you can.* If you've wondered why I'm giving you data to back up everything in this book, now you know why. I'm building your belief, thereby making everything you read more effective!

This is the perfect segue into the metaphysical rationale for how affirmations work:

- **Alignment with Quantum Potential:**[34] Affirmations in the present tense can align your conscious intentions with the quantum field of potentiality. By stating affirmations as if they are already true, you signal to the universe your readiness to manifest your desires in the present moment. This alignment is thought to enhance the likelihood of those desires materializing in your reality.

- **Resonance with Vibrational Frequencies:**[35] Metaphysically, affirmations are believed to emit vibrational frequencies aligned with your intentions. Stating affirmations in the present tense resonates with the idea that your current vibrational state is in harmony with your desired reality. This resonance is thought to attract similar vibrational experiences, drawing your goals closer to your current existence.

- **Merging with the Eternal Now:**[36] Affirmations in the present tense can be seen as a practice of merging your consciousness with the eternal now, transcending linear time. In this metaphysical view, the past and future are seen as existing simultaneously with the present. Affirming your desires as already true is a way to tap into this timeless realm, where manifestation can occur beyond the constraints of conventional time.

- **Cocreation with the Divine:**[37] Some metaphysical beliefs suggest that affirmations in the present tense are a form of cocreation with the divine or universal intelligence. By affirming your desires in the present moment, you align your will with the divine, inviting synchronicities and opportunities that facilitate the manifestation of your goals.

From the metaphysical perspective, affirmations are not just psychological tools but also spiritual and quantum practices that engage with the fabric of reality itself. (More on the quantum and how to use it in the next chapter.) Affirmations are a way to harmonize your consciousness with the infinite possibilities of the universe and to invite the divine and quantum forces to work in your favor.

Now that you understand why affirmations aren't new-age nonsense, here's how you can build a bridge of self-belief while using the creative power of your words.

Imagine a positive affirmation you'd like to confidently state about yourself. To demonstrate, I'm going to use this affirmation: "I deeply love and accept myself."

Now, if you don't feel that way, your subconscious is going to call bullshit. You'll feel the dissonance rather than the resonance, and that's not helpful. So, you can do one of two things.

Option 1: You can reframe it into a declaration. That might sound something like, "I have the ability to learn to deeply love and accept myself."

Or …

Option 2: You can shift the affirmation into one your mind can get behind. Dr. Jenn taught me this, and it's a 10/10. Here's how:

Instead of saying something you don't feel or believe, in this example, "I deeply love and accept myself," we're going to add a few words to the beginning.

Now it becomes, "I *am the type of person who can* deeply love and accept myself."

If that still feels untrue, add a few words to the beginning again:

"I *am willing to consider that* I am the type of person who can deeply love and accept myself."

In my experience personally and with coaching clients, this last statement can stretch far enough to build a sturdy bridge between where you are now, and where you're trying to go. Remember—the journey of a thousand miles begins with a single step.

Tomorrow never comes. I feel compelled to remind you of this truth. You've waited long enough. You'll never feel ready. It'll never be the perfect time. But here's some good news: You *are* ready! You've *been* ready. *It is your season. It is your time!*

You can't see the picture when you're in the frame. Step outside of it to see the bigger picture of your life and your impact. Will your legacy be one of service, priorities honored, dreams pursued, and realized potential? Or not? The choice is yours. For what it's worth, I believe in you.

COMMIT

Recall your imagined eulogy at the end of a long, happy, fulfilling life where you made the most of your time here. If it feels aligned, make a commitment to yourself, right here and now.

The magic of committing *intentionally* is who you'll become along the way. This is the exact process I used to begin transforming into my Higher Self. I still use it *every day* because this process never ends! But *in process* is a happy place to be, because you release more happy neurochemicals like dopamine in pursuit of a goal than you do upon achieving it.[38]

Committing to bringing forth your Higher Self and the actions to become her will make your self-confidence soar. I've heard it said that self-confidence comes from keeping promises to ourselves. This is what gets the snowball rolling down the mountain until it creates an avalanche. Imagine who you'll be and what you'll be able to do when you become a woman of your word *to yourself.*

There are a few ways to commit to bringing forth your Higher Self. One I recommend is signing a contract. You can fill in and sign the commitment contract I've provided here inside the book, or you can go to alessiacitro.com/book to download and print it out.

Before I began writing this book, my book coach, Jake Kelfer, encouraged me to sign a commitment contract. He then invited me to post it on social media for extra accountability. I did both—and now here you are reading the creation that came from that commitment. (If you print, sign, and post this, please tag me on Instagram at @alessiacitro__ so I can cheer you on!) Commitment moves mountains. You got this, sis.

> I, [your name] _____,
> commit to becoming my Higher Self!
> I commit to making myself a priority.
> I commit to bringing forth my gifts to the world.
> I commit to owning my identity as a divine child of God / the universe / a Higher Power.
> I commit to keeping an open mind and open heart.

I commit to learning to fall in love with the process.

I commit to having ears to hear and eyes to see as miracles begin unfolding all around me, and I intend to notice them.

I commit to creating a positive ripple effect in the world, simply by being the best version of me.

Signed: _____

Date: _____

Now, put your hand over your heart and say this aloud: "I commit to becoming my Higher Self!"

Then touch your head with your index finger and say: "I have everything within me to BE HER NOW!"

BE HER NOW EXERCISE:

Every journey is more fun with friends! Who is a friend or connection who's on the same page as you in wanting to step into her Higher Self? And who in that category will also *hold you to doing it*? Text that person right now and ask them to hold you accountable to finishing this book and applying what you learn. Better yet, invite them to do it with you.

Chapter 9

Be Her Now: The Power of the Quantum

"The core of my being is the ultimate reality, the root and ground of the universe, the source of all that exists."

—Deepak Chopra

WE ARE MADE OF STARDUST

It's true. And it's not just poetic; it's physics. We're all connected. Not only to each other, but to the universe and everything in it, and it goes way deeper than what we can see. This connection underpins the realm of quantum mechanics. If you feel slightly intimidated upon reading "quantum mechanics," stick with me while we break it down. It's about the incredibly small stuff that makes up *everything* and is less complicated than it sounds. Understanding what follows will provide a powerful and unique perspective of your potential for growth and transformation. It will empower you to understand how aligning your heart and mind can change your life.

Imagine that everything around you is built with LEGOS. The LEGOS are made up of tinier components called atoms. Think of atoms like the dots in a pointillist painting. Recall the *Ferris Bueller's Day Off* scene where Ferris, Sloane, and Cameron venture to The Art Institute of Chicago. Cameron stares at the famous Georges Seurat pointillist masterpiece, A *Sunday Afternoon on the Island of La Grande Jatte*, as the camera zooms in on the artwork until you can see the dots that make up the larger picture. You, and everything you see, are like the Seurat painting—it's tiny components that create the whole. Seeing the world in this way, as building blocks made of atoms, is Isaac Newton's old-school model of reality. Then Einstein came along and said, "Hold up, y'all. There's more to the story." Okay, he didn't really say that, but he did give us a new paradigm that opened the doors to the quantum.

In the quantum realm, things get weird in a good way. This view of reality is that everything is made of particles even smaller than atoms. These particles can be linked together (or *entangled*), even when vast distances apart, They can become entangled in different ways. Sometimes they share a common origin, like photons being split from the same atom. Other times, they may collide and interact, thereby establishing a connection. Once they're entangled, they will mirror the other's behavior identically and instantaneously, regardless of the distance between them. Einstein called this "spooky action at a distance." Kind of like using your phone's Nest app to instantly change your home's thermostat even if you're across the world, imagine two toy cars operated by the same remote control app. If you move one car forward, the other will do the same thing instantaneously, no matter how far apart they are because they share this connection. Not a perfect example, but this is how entangled particles interact. When entangled, they are synchronized.

What's more, these particles have a dual nature. When *observed*, they appear at a specific location and behave like a tiny point of matter. But when not observed, they behave more like a wave, existing in a state of potential and probability rather than as material in a definite location. Imagine playing "freeze dance" as a little kid. You'd be moving and grooving until told to "freeze." Observation is like calling out "freeze" to the wave function of a particle. It collapses the wave, causing the particle to take on a definite location and material properties.

This is critical for what follows, so let's put it another way. Until conscious observation causes a wave of potential and probability to collapse into a particle with definitive properties and location, that particle exists in a *superposition* state—meaning *it can be multiple places simultaneously*. This can be difficult to wrap your mind around initially—but think of it like this. You are like the particle. And superposition is akin to the infinite possibilities and outcomes for your life. What you give your attention and focus to (what you choose to *observe*) collapses these infinite possibilities into your definite, lived reality.

We all know people whose sunny disposition seems to bring about favorable circumstances. We've all seen or experienced firsthand how our directed focus and energy yields results. Sure, this is the RAS at work, but it's also the quantum. (Everything is connected anyway, so what if the RAS is a gateway to leverage the quantum field?) Now you know the reason for this phenomenon. What if this isn't "woo-woo," new-age BS? What if it's quantum mechanics at work on a macroscopic level? *What desired reality can you direct your intention and focus to, to bring it into material reality?*

There's one more underpinning of the quantum that's important before we talk about application. While we can direct our focus and attention to desired realities, some unpredictability and uncertainty will always remain. In quantum terms, this is known as the Heisenberg Uncertainty Principle. It states that there are certain properties of a particle that can't be measured at the same exact time. What this means relative to our lives is that we cannot focus, concentrate, and observe our way to certainty and specific outcomes across the breadth of our human experience. Sorry to disappoint my fellow control freaks! Focus on what truly matters, and stay open to the unexpected and spontaneous. Let the universe surprise and delight you.

CONNECTED MINDS

Back to entanglement and how we're all connected. We're all made of stardust, which is quite literally where the elements in our bodies come from. Nearly all the elements that build everything around us were formed in the heart of stars. When those stars grew old and exploded, they spread these elements across the universe. Those bits of star stuff eventually came together to make planets, including Earth and everything on it, including us. We're entangled and connected because we have a shared origin. You might be thinking, *Cool story—but how can I use this to enhance my reality and society?*

In 1987, Dr. Jacobo Grinberg-Zylberbaum conducted an experiment, venturing into the realm of human consciousness to explore its potential quantum underpinnings.[39] Individuals meditated in pairs while their brain waves were measured with an electroencephalograph (EEG) device. Some pairs of meditators demonstrated a mental link, meaning their brain wave patterns were correlated. They could feel when they were in *direct communication* with each other. In the experiment, *direct communication* was defined as "an interaction which occurs when subjects are able to feel each other's presence without the use of any sensory stimuli." The EEG measurements confirmed the meditators' feelings of connectedness.

These connected individuals were then separated into soundproof, electromagnetically insulated chambers. While maintaining their *direct communication*, only one of the individuals was exposed to bright flashes of light and auditory stimuli. Researchers observed a phenomenon akin to quantum entanglement. The brain of the unstimulated participant mirrored the response of the stimulated one! This experiment suggests that the principles of quantum mechanics, particularly entanglement, extend into the domain of human consciousness, hinting at a deep interconnectedness of minds. If you've ever felt like you read someone's mind (or they read yours), you weren't imagining it!

This is a great opportunity to revisit the HeartMath study referenced at the very beginning of this book. By aligning heartfelt intention with elevated emotions, participants trained to enter a state of heart coherence could wind or unwind DNA through intention—whether they held the test tube in their hands or held the intention from a half-mile away.

The implications for connecting to your own heartfelt intentions, pairing them with aligned emotions, and acting in accordance is a powerful way to manifest changes in your reality. Now imagine doing this in community with like-minded individuals whom you feel connected to. There is a reason the name for groups like this is a *mastermind*. Bringing together connected minds in these elevated states is a means of accessing higher levels of being and the accompanying experiences. This isn't only about changing *your* life for the better. This intentional way of connected living helps society too. One example: A transcendental meditation group lowered crime in Washington, DC by 23.3 percent, with the rates improving as the group grew larger.[40] There's power in our collective consciousness. Let's put it to good use.

HEALING THE PAST

Now that you understand how we can leverage the quantum field to create reality, let's take it up a notch with a study that blew my mind when I read about it in Dr. Joe Dispenza's *Breaking the Habit of Being Yourself.*[41]

In 2000, Dr. Leonard Leibovici conducted a study to test the effectiveness of prayer.[42] Specifically, could prayer speed up healing for people who were already sick? To find out, the researchers looked at a group of 3,393 patients admitted to an Israeli hospital with blood infections. These patients were randomly split into two groups: an intercession group that would be prayed for and a control group that would not receive prayer. The patients in the intercession group did not know they were being prayed for.

Regarding mortality rates, both groups had similar outcomes, too close to have statistical significance. Of the prayed-for (intercession) group, 28.1 percent passed away, compared to 30.2 percent of the group that wasn't prayed for (the control group).

However, a statistically significant difference in outcomes *was* seen when it came to fever duration and days spent in the hospital. Prayed-for patients got out of the hospital faster. The prayed-for group also had a significantly shorter duration of fever.

Here's where this study becomes mind-bending ... and time-bending. *The prayers for the intercession group were said after the patients were hospitalized with infection—four to ten years after these patients had been hospitalized with infection!* Yes, you read that correctly. *Praying for patients who had been sick years prior affected their healing ... in the past.*

I know, it's hard to believe. A few more details for the skeptics (which included me). *All* adult patients with a detected bloodstream infection at Israel's Rabin Medical Center Beilinson Campus between 1990 and 1996 were included in this study. (Did you think it was strange that over 3,000 people were at the same hospital with a blood infection? Now you know why—they weren't there simultaneously.) The patients on the list were assigned to the intercession or control group using a random number generator. Their health outcomes had already happened, and their files didn't change. Their hospital stay length and fever duration outcomes showed a statistically significant difference from the control group because *their healing was affected by prayers that happened four to ten years later.* If you need to read this multiple times to get your mind around it, don't worry—I did too. (As an aside, I can't help but wonder if the mortality rates between the two groups would have been statistically significant as well, had those praying for the intercession group been trained in heart coherence techniques to make their intention and prayers even more powerful.)

So, if prayer can affect and change the past, how could it affect and heal past, present, and thus future versions of you? What could prayer or focused intention do to create the life and version of yourself that you desire?

BE HER NOW AND 3D PRINT YOUR DESIRED REALITY

Let's put this all together and tie it with a bow. What does this quantum stuff mean for us on a practical level in terms of becoming our Higher Selves?

Quantum law dictates that all possibilities coexist across space and time until observation occurs. Now, think of this regarding personal growth. By making peace with your past and staying focused and intentional in the present, we guide our actions and decisions to align with our goals and values. It's through this focused attention and action that we *observe* our desired reality. This collapses possibility into the definitive, thereby shaping our future.

Forgiveness and how we perceive our past—and how we choose to feel about it—can effectively *heal* the past, changing how we feel and act in the present, leading to a better future. It's like using a spotlight to illuminate only the paths we want to walk down, leaving the others in the dark. By consistently focusing on the outcomes we desire, we're more likely to act in alignment and move toward them.

Perhaps this is the science behind *the eternal moment of now* and the power of gratitude. When you're grateful, you're in the present. You're at peace with the past, even temporarily, knowing it got you where you are. Gratitude also opens you to the possibilities of the future. Being grateful for your desired future as if it's already happened is a key to manifestation. So, becoming your Higher Self is as simple as *being her now*. Feel the gratitude for her now. Implement her habits now. Act as if you're her, *now*. The mere act of embodying her means you are observing your desired future, causing that possibility to "collapse" into definiteness. When you *be* her, you *are* her.

Let's underscore something you may have picked up on. In the quantum field, time and space are more like suggestions than hard rules. This is where visualization can help supercharge transformation and help you (your ego, specifically) resist it less. Visualization makes the future familiar, and familiar is comfortable. Remember, your subconscious mind loves comfort and familiarity. When you visualize being your Higher Self, you create a "quantum blueprint." This blueprint exists beyond time and space constraints, guiding the universe to align your current reality with your envisioned one. Visualizing and emotionally aligning to your Higher Self need not be time-consuming or elaborate. In the next chapter, I'll take you through a quick and simple guided visualization to do this, the substance of which you'll be able to easily revisit wherever and whenever needed, whether it's in line at the post office or out on a walk.

Remember that in the quantum realm, things happen instantaneously, even if they don't show up in our 3D reality at the same speed. By taking aligned action, as if you are already the version of yourself you wish to be, you're not just sending the message to the universe that you're ready. You're becoming an active participant in making that blueprint a reality. The quantum field doesn't distinguish between the blueprint and reality; it simply aligns them by collapsing probability and potential into definitive reality through your continued focus, intention, and action (observation). The more you embody and align with this version of you, the more you pull that reality into your current experience.

When you *be her now*, you're not waiting for a future moment; you're recognizing that you have the power to literally *bring the future to you*. The more you embrace this, the more your external world will reflect this new reality. Do this enough, and you will 3D print the life of your dreams.

BE HER NOW REFLECTION:

Now that you understand the enormous power of our intention, focus, and the quantum field, what feelings and possibilities are stirred within you? Are you excited? Nervous about this magical power you didn't realize you possessed? Are you wanting to change the world? I invite you to journal on this and explore what you are most looking forward to creating, now that you possess this knowledge and know how to apply it.

Chapter 10
Higher Self Identity

"We delight in the beauty of the butterfly, but rarely admit the changes it has gone through to achieve that beauty."

—Maya Angelou

IDENTITY GOVERNS EVERYTHING

My best friend Shannon got married in the heart of South Africa's renowned wine country. Not quite a year into sobriety at the time, I was interested to see how I'd feel being surrounded by some of the world's best wines—and not partaking. To my delight, I was not even remotely tempted. There was no trace of FOMO. I realized it was because I had changed my identity. It's not that I *can't* drink. It's that I *don't* drink. I absolutely could have, but since I no longer identify as a drinker, why would I?

Think for a moment about the version of you that you're aspiring to be. This is your desired identity. Are you *identifying* as that version yet? Are you looking at this next-level you as a fantasy or an optional upgrade? Or have you *decided* and committed to becoming her?

Decide is derived from the Latin word *decider* ("determine"), from *de-* ("off") and *caedere* ("cut"). Once you decide you're leveling up, you *cut off* all the bullshit and excuses you previously entertained. You take on your new identity and let it govern everything—with ease and energy savings.

Truly, one of the best parts of stepping into a new identity is how much energy it frees up. Back to the drinking example— do you know how much energy it took when I was attempting to moderate? To choose whether or not I was going to drink? To try to calculate if I'd had too much or if I could order another? Whether I'd be good to drive when it was time to head home? It was exhausting! I didn't realize it until I quit for good. And I'm willing to bet you're doing this in an area of your life right now. What is something you're waffling and wasting energy on that could be decided once and for all with a permanent identity upgrade?

This is the part of the process where you meet and align with your Higher Self. It's time to bring your logical mind into agreement with your heart and soul, which already know what is possible and meant for you.

As you read this chapter and begin to create your Higher Self identity, please remember this: It's good to feel good, and "we change best by feeling good, not by feeling bad."[43] I say this because as discussed in a previous chapter, it can be easy to fixate on the gap between where we are today and where we want to go. If you feel miles apart from the identity you desire, remember how far you've come and feel incredible about it. Look at all you're capable of. You just read a chapter on quantum mechanics! How's that for supporting evidence? Remember, too, envisioning our Higher Selves is not a perfectionist pursuit. It is about coming into the remembrance of the potential and divine within us and uncovering this version at the pace that's right for you.

YOU'RE GOLDEN, GIRL

Reflect for a moment about what lies within you. I'd go so far as to say there's pure gold in there, just waiting to be rediscovered. Take the following true story as a metaphor for your own true nature.

In 1955, a large Buddha statue was being relocated to a new building within the Wat Traimit temple in Bangkok, Thailand. While the temple's monks were moving it, the statue was accidentally dropped, causing some of it to break off. The horror of breaking this statue was short-lived because the break revealed a glimmer—of gold. Curious, the monks carefully removed more plaster, ultimately revealing a solid gold Buddha weighing about 6 tons.

When I first heard this story, I wondered why anyone would cover up a magnificent, solid gold statue. The answer, of course, is the same reason we cover up our own gold—for protection. It's believed that in the eighteenth century, the statue was covered in a thick layer of stucco to prevent it from being stolen and destroyed during the Burmese invasions that took place in that period. All the temple's monks were killed by invaders or fled. The truth was lost until the statue was dropped and broken, two hundred years later. If you feel broken right now, perhaps it's just what you need to uncover your gold.

MEET YOUR HIGHER SELF

We're going to use several tools for you to come to know your Higher Self. In fact, you'll know her so well by the time you finish this book that you'll be able to call on her for intuitive guidance whenever needed. It took me a while to really strengthen this muscle (and I'm still working on it daily), but my Higher Self has become a very reliable adviser. It feels extraordinarily good to trust my own knowing for the first time since childhood. Now it's your turn!

Journaling

To prepare the way to meet your Higher Self, journaling by putting pen to paper is one of the most effective exercises you can do. Writing by hand activates the brain in a way that typing does not, allowing you to access more of your subconscious mind and creativity.

Handwriting engages complex motor skills and activates various brain regions, including those associated with memory and learning. The precise hand movements involved, along with the associated visual and proprioceptive feedback, significantly enhance the brain's connectivity patterns and engage the brain more deeply, essential for learning and memory.[44]

Journaling can also help you process emotions and improve your health. One study found that journaling about emotional experiences significantly reduces doctor visits, improves immune markers, improves school and work outcomes, and lowers stress levels.[45]

Since reading *The Artist's Way* by Julia Cameron in my Soul Sisters Book Club, I've taken to the practice of Morning Pages. You write your unfiltered stream of consciousness for three pages first thing every morning. The connections I make in these pages that would otherwise have escaped me are amazing. There's also something to be said for doing this in the morning before being fully awake and alert. Right after waking, your brain may still be producing theta waves, the state linked to creativity, intuition, and access to subconscious thoughts and memories.[46] This can help access insights and thoughts that may be out of reach while in more alert states dominated by alpha and beta waves.

Regardless of the time of day you choose to journal, consider this your invitation to grab a beautiful new notebook that you can't wait to write in.

Visualization

This is one of my favorite tools, and an incredibly powerful one because your brain doesn't know the difference between real and vividly imagined experiences.

A study by University College London researchers suggests the more vividly a person imagines something, the more likely they are to believe it's real.[47] The study investigated how the brain differentiates between imagination and reality. Participants were asked to imagine images while looking at a computer screen. When real images were gradually introduced, participants believed their imagination had become more vivid. The study concluded that the brain has difficulty distinguishing between real and imagined experiences, especially when the imagined experiences are vivid. This is attributed to overlapping brain circuits used for both imagination and perception.

An important note: When you do any visualization, ensure it's not a 2D, flat imagining. The more real and textured you can make the internal experience, the more effective it will be. Imagine sounds, smells, tastes, textures, and especially emotions.

The more clearly and detailed you can imagine your Higher Self, the more she will become your reality ... and the more you'll become her.

To help you get to know her, below is a guided visualization you can use that takes about five minutes. You can go to alessiacitro.com/book to access a free recording, or you can record yourself speaking the text below and then play it back. Do whatever feels the most aligned and supportive to you. Come back to this recording as often as you'd like until your vision of your Higher Self is crystal clear.

Tips before beginning:

- Have some water close by. It'll help you come back into your body when the visualization concludes.
- Have a notebook handy. At the end, write down anything that stands out from the experience.
- Access this however it works for you. I worked with a client who could not access visual imagination due to a condition called aphantasia. Upon further research, there are other conditions that can also make visualization inaccessible. If you have one of these conditions, you get to play too! Instead of listening and imagining visually, use the text below as an extended journal prompt and leverage sensory and emotional engagement.

GUIDED VISUALIZATION

Set an intention for your authentic wisdom to guide and lead you to your Higher Self.

Take a deep breath and gently feel your body. Feel your feet on the ground and your body in the chair. If you're lying down, feel your body being supported by the ground below you.

As you breathe in and out, feel how held you are by the Earth. Feel its supportive energy, and how through Mother Earth, you are connected to all the women who have come before you and who will come after. Call any supportive energies to come and be with you now. Feel into this support and safety and soften a bit more.

Now invite your authentic wisdom to find a space that's going to be the perfect meeting place for you and your Higher Self. It could be a place in nature, a temple, a palace, a library, anywhere. Go with your first impression. If you're more kinesthetic, it may be a feeling. If you're auditory, it may be hearing a story, a song, or a melody. It may be a combination of all these.

Allow your authentic wisdom to begin choosing and bringing up this safe place, where it's easy to be supported in connecting to your Higher Self.

Imagine as you step into this place, that off to one side, there is a large, alchemic fire with flames that can transmute and transform. On the other side, there is an ocean of water filled with healing energies.

However this is showing up for you is perfect. Observe and allow whatever comes up.

As you step toward this meeting place, offer whatever your authentic wisdom knows needs to be cleared or healed to the ocean and to the fire. You may not consciously be aware of what is going into the fire and into the ocean, but trust that whatever needs to be cleared is being cleared. With every outbreath, you are releasing and letting go.

Relax your jaw. Release your hands. Imagine letting it all go and releasing what is meant to be let go of morc and more with every breath.

You are creating more and more space for you to access your authentic wisdom and meet your Higher Self.

When you're ready, imagine you're moving into the meeting space that your authentic wisdom has selected.

Invite your authentic wisdom to present as your Higher Self, in whatever way will be most supportive for you now. Notice and allow whatever is arising.

When you're ready, open to whatever you're meant to learn, feel, or understand. Notice and observe her. What is she wearing? How does she look? What is her energy like? How does her aura make you feel?

Ask your Higher Self, what does she need from you to support deepening your connection? What do you need from her to go deeper? How can you hear, feel, and trust her guidance? How can you both support your good and the highest good of all by deepening your communication and connection? How can you access this whenever you desire?

What do you want to ask her? Ask your Higher Self, what message does she have for you today?

Ask your Higher Self to merge with you now. Ask for her and your authentic wisdom to remain with you and to be available to be called upon.

As you get ready to leave this sacred meeting place and part ways, do whatever feels supportive, whether it's an embrace, an exchange of words, or anything else that wants to come up. Take another moment now, and turn to walk out the same way you came in. Notice and observe how you feel. What's changed?

Begin to wiggle your fingers and toes. When you're ready, begin to open your eyes. Look around the room to come back into the environment. If you have a drink close by, take a sip. You can rub your face or touch your arms. Tap each shoulder with the opposite hand to create right and left integration. Come back into your environment.

BE HER NOW REFLECTION:

What came up for you during this visualization? Spend as much time as you need to journal the details and anything else that feels important.

ZERO IN ON THE TARGET

Now that you've seen who you are as your most authentic, Highest Self, let's clarify your aspirations. This is also a tactic in behavior design which we'll address in Chapter 18. We must have a clear aspiration or outcome we are working toward. Without this, we'll spin our wheels, grow frustrated, and give up. You can't hit a target that hasn't been established.

For example, I aspire to be a present and loving mother and wife, a bestselling author, an in-demand speaker, and a leading high-performance coach ... "or something better," because I always leave the door open for the universe to surprise and delight. These aspirations are driven by my deeply rooted values of service, love, empowering others, and my mission to leave the world better than I found it.

So, in your mind's eye, who do you aspire to be? What's your dream? What's the vision on your heart? Without getting attached to specifics, what tangible outcomes would you like to manifest? When in doubt, expand on the personal mission statement you created in Chapter 4. Your mission and values comprise the changeless core you will continue building on and pivoting from. Let them serve as your compass.

If your aspirations are somewhat hazy, that's okay. Action breeds clarity. Trust that you'll get clearer and clearer as you get intentional and activated.

If your aspirations scare you, that's okay too. If your big vision doesn't scare you a little, it's not stretching you. And the magic happens in the growth zone! Remember, these changes won't happen overnight, even if they look that way to the outside world. You will gradually step into the new you and be prepared for your quantum leap when it takes place.

Chinese bamboo provides a beautiful metaphor here. A Chinese bamboo tree has no visible activity above ground for five years as it lays down its complex, deep root system. Then, in forty days, it grows up to ninety feet tall![48] Trust that even when it seems nothing is happening, *everything* is happening. By the time you reach your aspiration—you'll be ready.

UPGRADE YOUR IDENTITY

Your identity governs everything: your beliefs, perceptions, thoughts, emotions, actions, habits, and, thus, your reality. When you upgrade your identity, you upgrade your life.

Is that, perhaps, why we cling to the current (or even past) versions of us? Because we are so designed to resist change, even when it's positive? My mind immediately drew an analogy between the version of us it's time to shed and the mix of emotions and difficulty in ending a significant relationship. Recently, I wrote this in my journal:

Letting old versions of us go is like leaving a relationship when it's run its course. It doesn't mean it's easy. Or that you don't love that person. Or that you won't miss them. It means you've evolved to a point where that relationship fulfilled its purpose, and now it's time for what's next. Your love for that person (or that version of you) remains eternal. Let them go knowing this is true. When you take your next step, remember them with gratitude, knowing that without all you learned and who you became in that relationship, the step you now take with grace would've instead been an awkward leap across a gaping chasm.

It's like the adage, "We didn't come this far only to come this far." You're likely unrecognizable from who you were in high school, college, or your early twenties. You're not meant to stop evolving—and aren't you glad you haven't? So, why stop now? Whether we fulfill our potential or not, the world will keep turning. But when we take that first step and keep putting one foot in front of the other, we're giving a gift to ourselves and our souls, all those we're connected to (which is everyone), and we uplift the collective.

RAISE YOUR THERMOSTAT

Several years ago, I heard an episode of The Ed Mylett Show that I'd compare to being shaken awake. In the episode titled "Control Your Identity Change Your Life," Ed asserts that your identity functions like a thermostat. (For this example, let's say the higher the temperature, the more optimal.) Think of how the thermostat functions in your home. If it's cold out, the heater kicks on until it restores the temperature to its set point. If it's hot out, the air conditioning cools the space back down. Let's say your setting for wealth is at a comfortable 72 degrees, and you acquire 100 degrees worth of funds. Unless you change the thermostat to 100 degrees, you will find a way to lose, spend, gamble, or give 28 degrees away to get back to 72 degrees, where you're comfortable. This applies to any area of life: love, success, fitness, etc.

Here's a real-life example of the thermostat setting that many of you can relate to: my personal experiences with weight loss. Before I had my daughter, I was carrying twenty extra pounds around. Eight months after she'd been born, that weight was still there. I'd had enough of carrying it around like a handbag, so I hired a trainer at the end of July 2019. He gave me a strict nutrition plan that I followed to the letter. I did every workout he told me to. Three months later, I was the leanest I'd ever been. I'd lost twenty-eight pounds, and I looked and felt amazing.

Then, a year later, I gained most of it back. It'd be easy for me to blame the COVID pandemic and stress, but remember—we're victors, not victims.

At the beginning of 2021, I hired another trainer. She had a different approach, and I got great results again. This time, I lost about twenty pounds. And then, you guessed it—I gained most of it back ... again.

You probably know people who have had this yo-yo experience. Maybe you're one of them. And barring a medical reason, the weight finds its way back because the identity thermostat isn't set to maintain the leaner version. There may be contributing factors that make us want to keep a little extra weight on, consciously or not. In my case, a few extra pounds served as a form of protection and a way to be less visible—a trauma response. Factors like this affect the thermostat setting until we make peace with and release them.

It's the same reason behind phenomena you've experienced firsthand or through someone you know. A too-low identity thermostat is why your incredible best friend can't find the right partner despite being a total catch. It's why I've historically had a hard time holding onto money within my businesses—my identity has been that I'm "bad" with money. It's the reason you hear people say, "These things always happen to me." Sure, bad luck exists, but most of the time, we get what we believe we're worthy of and deserve. The worst part is that many of these defeating beliefs aren't even ours. If you were told you were stupid as a kid, you might believe you are, even though you have genius within. A lie told a thousand times becomes the truth. If you were to shed the lies, what would your truth be?

Remember at the beginning of this chapter when I mentioned aligning your heart and mind? This is why it matters. If your circumstances improve and you don't raise your internal set point (your thermostat setting) to match, you'll find a way to come back to where you're comfortable.

I have no doubt I'm triggering many of you here. And if I am, good. That's where the gold lies. We can't fix a problem until we are aware it exists and can name it. If you don't have the results you want in an area of your life, it's not a *you* problem. It's your thermostat setting. And it's within your control to change it.

Another factor that keeps our thermostats low can be the perverse belief that chronic struggle is noble. Why do we, as a culture, glorify hardship? Why do we believe that we can't be, do, and have with *ease* and with *joy*? We may even feel guilty when things are going well.

Obstacles can provide benefit because we'd never grow without anything to overcome, but how does it feel in your mind and body when things are flowing? You've likely noticed that when life is smooth sailing, there can sometimes be this nagging feeling that something's got to give. That the other shoe is going to drop. That's the Gambler's Fallacy sneaking in and lying to us. It's this idea that a streak of great days or "lucky" breaks is due to end. We're programmed to think that good fortune is a limited-time offer. But it doesn't have to be.

Perhaps you've even been the one to end your lucky streak because having things be so good was getting uncomfortable. I still do this in various ways, but I've grown my awareness to catch and correct it. If we have an internal limit for how good things can get, we may do something to bring ourselves back down to what's comfortable unless we work to remove the cap.

This is an invitation to begin eradicating the thought that struggling is noble and a requirement of life. The first step is expanding our capacity for goodness. Whether it's savoring the taste of chocolate, feeling the sun on your skin, smelling the fragrance on the breeze, seeing the smile of a child, hearing your favorite song, having your sides hurt from laughter, feeling the texture of grass under bare feet, or taking a relaxing bath—we must experience to expand our capacity for pleasure and abundance to have more of it.

As a mentor of mine, Dr. Valerie Rein says, let's strive for a life where we can't stop asking ourselves, *"How good can it get?"*

For now, I invite you to partake in the following reflection.

BE HER NOW REFLECTION:

- What areas of my life aren't where I want them to be?
- Have there been times when I've been flying high in a particular area, then come back down to the level I'd been at prior (or dropped even lower)?
- What is one limiting belief that's keeping my set point lower than I want it? Examine it and prepare to release it.
- What is one action I can take right now to raise my thermostat setting in an area where it's low? Some of my favorite ways to do this are indulging

in some of the free sensory activities listed above. Experiencing goodness begets more goodness. If it gets uncomfortable, use some of the tools we've discussed thus far: journaling, grounding into your body and giving a tour of your current reality to the parts of you being triggered, visualizing how your Higher Self would think, feel, and act, or envisioning your desired future and how this experience will get you closer to that reality.

Chapter 11

Higher Self Energetics

"The energy you bring, positive or negative, dictates your perceptions, receptions, and radiance."

—T. F. Hodge

A critical component of acting in alignment with our Higher Self is acting *in the energy of that identity.*

Imagine you've been gifted an exceptional bottle of wine. In fact, this particular wine and vintage is widely regarded as the very best in the world. You haven't opened and enjoyed it yet because you didn't feel ready and because there hadn't been an occasion special enough to justify doing so. But you've been reading this book and integrating its contents across your life. You know tomorrow never comes and that waiting until you're a sommelier isn't necessary for you to fully appreciate the masterpiece contained inside the bottle. So, you open it! Now you must choose a glass from which to drink this exceptional wine. Which do you select: a piece of beautiful crystal stemware, or a red Solo cup?

The answer is obvious. It's in the crystal where the wine is honored, its hues and bouquet allowed to dance into full expression. Similarly, you are the wine, rare and remarkable. Your energy and embodiment are the vessel into which you pour your talents, dreams, and essence. Do you see yourself as worthy of the crystal or the Solo cup? Will you honor or dim your inherent value?

You can "do the do" as your Higher Self, but if the energy you're showing up with is that of the self you're attempting to outgrow, you'll feel as though you're Sisyphus—rolling the boulder up the hill, only to have it roll back down—and you'll wonder why changes aren't taking root.

Most of us who grew up in consumerist Western culture were programmed under the false paradigm of *have, do, be.* For instance, once I *have* X, Y, or Z, I can *do* what will enable me to *be* happy, fulfilled, desired, successful, etc. Unfortunately, this is completely backward.

First, we must *be.* Arguably, our energetics matter more than anything we *do* when it comes to reaching a desired outcome. We've all experienced feeling someone's energy the moment they enter a room. If someone walks in with gravitas, you can feel it radiating off them. Likewise, if they walk in with doubt, worry, and franticness—you can feel that too. Who would you rather talk to at the party? Your energy matters.

Once we are *being* in alignment with our desired identity, anything we *do* will be in accordance with it. And voilà—at some point those actions will compound, and you'll *have* what you desire.

WHAT NOURISHES YOUR SOUL?

A great way to begin embodying your desired energy is to return to happy childhood moments.

Think about the last time you saw a child who was utterly blissful, silly, and carefree. My mind immediately goes to my daughter putting on a performance at an airport gate while we waited to board a flight. Almost five years old at the time, she was singing, dancing, and creating a contagion of joy in her midst. People near us were smiling, laughing, and genuinely happy to witness her in her element. If you've been to an airport lately, you know what a feat it is to spark joy in such an environment.

I've heard a reason why children are like this is because they're closer to the spiritual realm, having come from it more recently than the rest of us. Either way, most of us lose that joy and wonder as we get older. I have a hard time cutting loose like my daughter—even in private! But our childhood provides clues to what nourishes us.

Think back for a moment—what was something you could do for hours on end as a kid that you absolutely loved? Who were the friends you always wanted to play with and why? What was it that you did with them? How did they make you feel? What did you like to collect? Where did you most love spending time?

When I first did this exercise, many things began to make sense. I loved to draw, color, and read. I abandoned these hobbies completely until an existential crisis forced me to reexamine my life. Is it any wonder I felt blocked and encumbered after leaving my creativity behind as a relic of the past? I abandoned it to chase wealth and success in the analytical field of tech and wondered why I was so unhappy.

As you begin to rediscover these abandoned parts of yourself, approach them with curiosity. Avoid any expectation of being "good" at interests and hobbies when you revisit them. Watercolor painting did wonders for me on a soul level when

I picked it back up, even though the end result was far from a masterpiece. Indulging in the things we love can nourish us, whether or not we create something "good."

BE HER NOW ACTIVITY:

Take yourself and your inner child on a solo date this week. I began taking myself on solo dates in my mid-twenties while I lived in Chicago, and the reconnection to myself in these simple outings cannot be understated. Truly, it healed me in a difficult time. Go to a gallery, a museum, a crystal shop, a painting or pottery class, wine and dine yourself. Do whatever feels right or speaks to you—and go with your first idea!

VIBE CHECK YOURSELF

Ice Cube knew what was up when he released *Check Yo Self* in 1992. Regular vibe checks are necessary, or we'll wreck ourselves, especially as we step into our Higher Selves.

Imagine how your Higher Self shows up at the grocery store. Is she in a rush? Impatiently reaching around old ladies in the produce section so she can grab her organic arugula and get out of there? And I'm not judging because I've done this more times than I can count. Or, while embodying your Higher Self, are you showing up in a different energy—one of patience, grace, and poise, or however *your* Higher Self likes to roll?

It's one thing to know our energy precedes us and another to remember this while we're out in the world. But like anything, it can become automatic. And remember, we must! Our energy has implications in our real, lived experience, and if we don't take intentional ownership of it, we will continue to show up as though we're in a walking coma. We will stay reactive instead of becoming proactive in the creation of our lives.

Once we consciously embody our desired energy and get curious about it, we can create a pause and make different, more aligned choices. Going back to the grocery store example, I now set an intention to walk into Trader Joe's or Costco radiating love and patience—especially if it's a Sunday. (If you know, you know.) It may take me longer to get in and out of the store, but in this energy I enjoy being there, I smile more, and I have better interactions. It requires a shift, but it pays dividends. It's also an action with an immediate positive feedback loop, and you'll begin to crave the dopamine hit of carrying spacious energy out in the world.

Here's another reason to check your vibe. We are energetic beings. We are literally electric. Given this, we emit a certain frequency or vibration. This is what the law of attraction refers to with like attracting like.

Enter, the emotional frequency scale. Your emotions change your vibrational level. Created by Dr. David Hawkins, the emotional frequency scale is a hierarchal list of emotions, each with a numerical value representing its energy level, or frequency.[49] The scale ranges from one to one thousand. Lower numbers are tied to low-energy, negative states while higher numbers are representative of higher energy and positive states. (See Figure 11.1.)

What shocked me most when I learned about the scale is that the lowest frequency is shame, with guilt right above it. To vibrate lower than these, you'd need to be dead—and have no vibration.

Meanwhile, if you focus on feeling love, joy, and peace, you'll operate at the top of the scale. (The highest emotional frequency is enlightenment.) Remember, what you focus on expands. This is why having a gratitude practice is so huge. Put your RAS to work finding things to be grateful for, and your feelings of happiness and your vibration will increase with little to no effort. You'll magnetize more to be happy about and grateful for too.

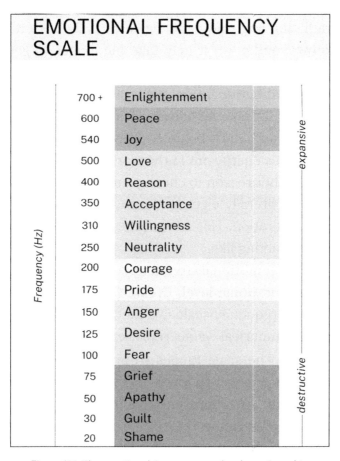

Figure 11.1: The emotional frequency scale, also referred to as the Map of Consciousness.

If you buy into magnetism and attracting vibrational matches, you can see why operating in states of anger, guilt, fear, etc., are sure ways to block your blessings and get more of what you don't want. This is not a call to repress your emotions. But it is a nudge to move through difficult emotions and transmute them. Look at the word *emotion*. It's energy ... in *motion*. Move it through and out via four methods that can be used together or separately: breath (deep breathing or breathwork), movement (dance, hitting a pillow, going on a run, etc.), sound (laughter, screams, sighs, yawns, chants, etc.), and tears.

Depending on the situation, one of my preferred methods of doing this is to acknowledge and feel my annoyance, anger, sadness, guilt, etc., and say to myself, "I choose to find and see the good." Every disadvantage has within it an equal seed of opportunity. Will you commit to being the type of person who seeks to find the seeds of opportunity?

BE HER NOW EXERCISE:

- Make a list of your favorite ways to experience pleasure and goodness. It can be sitting on a favorite park bench, putting your feet in the sand, or reading a book you love. The possibilities are endless. Of note, if your mind immediately went to sex when reading the word "pleasure," you're not alone, and it's a sure sign you need nonsexual pleasure (or maybe more of both?) in your life.

- Write down ten pleasurable actions and keep revisiting and adding to this list until you have created a broad Pleasure Menu (shoot for at least twenty-five items).
- For the next week, pick *one* item on your Pleasure Menu to experience each day. Rate your capacity for pleasure on Day 1 on a scale of one to ten. Rate yourself again at the end of the week. Did your capacity for pleasure expand?

EMBODYING EMOTION

We are triune beings (mind, body, and soul). Because of modern life, most of us have developed a disconnection between these three parts of ourselves.

First, let's discuss the mind and body disconnection. I was with a coaching client recently and asked her how a particular experience made her feel *in her body*. Her response was not uncommon. It was along the lines of, "I'm anxious, I'm nervous, I'm sad, etc." We touched on this in Chapter 7 about fears, but it bears repeating because it is deeply ingrained in most of us. We can name an emotion, but we usually don't *feel* it. What's more, as we talked about earlier, our wording typically suggests we *identify* with the emotion ("I am sad") instead of *feeling* a state that is transitory in nature ("I feel sad").

So, how can we begin to embody a feeling instead of labeling or identifying as it? The first question to ask yourself is, where do you *feel it in your body*? What color is it? What is the texture? What does it look like? Is it solid, liquid, gas? Does it move and morph or is it static? How much space would it take up if it wanted to expand? I get playful and curious as I move through these questions. And they're effective because they create distance, just like we did with Pam. We are no longer our emotions, just like we are no longer our negative inner voice.

WHAT DOES YOUR YES FEEL LIKE?

Everything in this chapter is meaningless if we are unable to connect into our own truth. And the more we tune in to truth and what it *feels like in the body*, the more we will begin to trust our decisions. Here is a simple way to begin reconnecting to the feeling of your truth.

State a known, indisputable fact and note internal resonance. For example, say, "My name is [your name]" and note the feeling. Now try it again, but with a name that is *not* yours. Did you notice the difference? If not, keep trying with other pieces of objectively factual information—like what you'd use for a security question when creating an account on a highly secure website. For example, the city, state, or country you live in, where you were born, or your mother's name. Like everything in this book, approach it with curiosity and see what you feel when you compare facts to falsehoods. A feeling of *resonance* is the feeling of truth, and *dissonance* is the feeling of falsehood.

DON'T FORGET TO HAVE FUN

As we close Part Two on Alignment, don't forget to make this process fun and enjoyable. Imagine that living life in your full expression as your Higher Self is a game you *get to* play—because it is!—and that just by playing, you've already won.

BE HER NOW REFLECTION:

What emotions does your Higher Self embody? What are the natural emotional states she gravitates to?

Part Three: Audit

"The unexamined life is not worth living."

—Socrates

Chapter 12

Put Out the Fire to Clear the Smoke

"In order to step into a new future, you must first confront the parts of you that aren't going there."

—Dr. Joe Dispenza

When it comes to change and improvement, we often stay in sameness because we're unsure where to start. This chapter will begin to illuminate where to begin.

Auditing is all about examining life's primary areas and noting where changes and improvements can be made. Auditing your life probably sounds as enjoyable as a root canal, but don't worry—you'll be given a framework to make it simple and straightforward. This stage of the process happens to be my favorite because of the clarity and subsequent freedom it brings.

This is a good time for a few reminders:

- Slow and steady wins the race.
- All-or-nothing is no longer your MO.
- Small changes compound into *huge* results, at a rate that is right for you.

- Tap into your inner authority and trust your YES, *and* your NO.

As you read this part of the book, know I'm doing this alongside you. My life has improved a whole hell of a lot, but it's far from "perfect." I'm continually needing to audit and edit over here. It can be easy to get caught up in all the areas we have yet to master, but focusing on the progress we've already made is extremely supportive and grounding to both our confidence and sense of possibility. As you go through the next chapters, I invite you to focus on how well you're already doing, not on what needs "fixing." When an area of opportunity is staring you in the face as your starting point, how can you approach it with genuine curiosity rather than self-judgment?

As you consider your own audit, do not think for one moment that you need to do *everything*. And certainly not all at once. That's a recipe for doing nothing. Years ago, I saw an integrative nutritionist who gave me a twenty-page report with changes to make. Guess how many changes I implemented? Yep—*zero*. I was overwhelmed, in analysis paralysis, and I archived the email ... forever. Don't fall into this trap of thinking you must do everything. You don't.

View what follows like a menu. Find your starting point and come back to choose additional items later when you're ready to dig in again. You may find it helpful or supportive to add sticky tabs or bookmarks to the audit areas that resonate with you so you can easily find them again. When we get into the next part of the book, *Activate*, I'll teach you how to design behaviors that create lasting habits, and how to narrow in on which specific behaviors to start with.

A final note before we jump into the meat of this chapter. The solution is rarely as simple as "drink more water" or "get more sleep." It's always deeper. If it weren't, you wouldn't have bought a book for a holistic approach to habits.

I will blend several different schools of thought and paradigms in this chapter, for two reasons. One, different parts will speak to different people. Take what you need and file away the rest. Two, seeing the overlap between these different perspectives will help you start connecting the dots within your life. Everything is interconnected, if only we are open to seeing it that way. We're going to start basic and end by bringing it all together.

YOUR HIERARCHY OF NEEDS

Think about a time you were incredibly stressed. Perhaps you had a five-alarm financial situation, a severely ill family member, fallout from a natural disaster, etc. Now imagine something less catastrophic that was still stressful. Maybe it was a big, high-stakes project at work, a fight with your partner (maybe because you were "hangry" ... not that I'm speaking from experience), or a time you were late for school pickup. While you were in those situations—in a level of fight, flight, or freeze—were you concerned about your personal development? No. Because your needs have a hierarchy, or an order, in which they must be met and addressed.

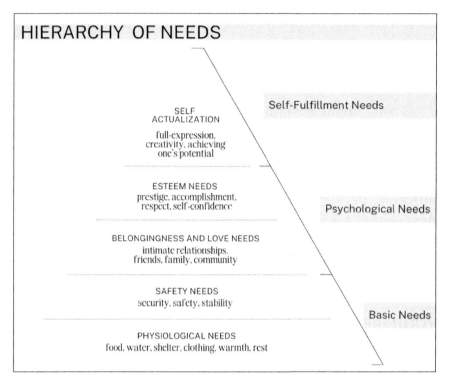

Figure 12.1: Maslow's Hierarchy of Needs

Enter Maslow's Hierarchy of Needs, conceived by psychologist Abraham Maslow in the mid-twentieth century. It presents a prioritization framework for understanding human needs and motivations. Visualized as a pyramid with five distinct levels (see Figure 12.1), this model offers insights into the progression of human requirements.

At its foundational tier, the base of the pyramid, are physiological needs. These encompass essentials for survival like hydration, adequate nutrition, shelter, and clothing. Ascending the pyramid to the next level, safety needs come into focus. These include stability, safety, and security. Think financial stability, a stable home environment, and living in a safe neighborhood or a country in peacetime. The third level is emotional needs—specifically the need for love and belonging—which encompass interpersonal relationships, family, friendships, and a sense of belonging within communities. Continuing upward, we arrive at self-esteem needs. These include the need for competence, self-respect, recognition, and the pursuit of personal accomplishments. Maslow's hierarchy culminates with the concept of self-actualization, where we strive for personal growth, self-fulfillment, and realizing our inherent potential.

It's a common observation that personal development tends to be a pursuit more prevalent among the affluent. This is partly because it can be challenging to explore your full potential when worrying about stability or basic human needs. As the saying goes, you'd have bigger fish to fry.

When you look at your own life, which areas closest to the pyramid's base need addressing first? If you're a mom, adequate sleep might be a basic need that's not regularly met. Or perhaps you tend to get busy with work and meetings, and you forget to eat lunch or don't have a free moment to do so. Are you drinking enough water? Do you feel safe in your home and at work? You can know everything there is to know about habits and behavior design, but if you are struggling to shore up a basic need, you will have a difficult time making progress—and keeping it.

Of note, solidifying the first three levels of the pyramid is essential to experiencing a feeling of harmony. Otherwise, you may feel like you're playing Whac-A-Mole with one area of your life firing on all cylinders while the others suffer. I experienced this frequently before finding harmony though habits. One area would suddenly require immediate attention and correction, and I'd shift my focus to put the fire out, causing the previously strong area to fall into disarray. Maybe you can relate! Focusing on basics is like going slow to go fast later. We want to build our Higher Self Habits on steel, not sand.

Here's the great news. In one sense, having our needs met is like playing Jenga. If you build higher by taking resources from below and weaken the foundation, eventually the tower will fall. But unlike Jenga, you can pull from the top and shore up the bottom. You can pull resources and strength from upper levels to solidify the ones below. This might look like receiving divine inspiration and creating a life-changing product that pulls you out of poverty. It might be using your skills and capability to create community and security. Perhaps its love carrying you through a phase where you're fighting to survive. Wherever you're weakest, look up to source the solution.

THE OVERLAP BETWEEN BRAIN LAYERS AND THE NEEDS HIERARCHY

Remember how we talked about neuroscience in Chapter 5 and how, if we're unaware, our brain's architecture can limit us? There's overlap here that provides more insight. First, here's a quick refresher on what we discussed in Chapter 5.

There are three layers to the brain: the reptilian brain, the limbic system, and the neocortex.

The reptilian brain is tasked with basic survival functions like breathing, heart rate, and the like. The limbic system is the brain's emotional center, responsible for emotions, memory, and motivation. The third layer is the neocortex, and within it is the prefrontal cortex. The prefrontal cortex is what differentiates humans from all other species. It is responsible for higher-order thinking, problem-solving, language, and conscious decision-making.

Our base layer of the brain, often referred to as the "reptilian" brain, directly corresponds to the two base layers of Maslow's hierarchy pyramid: physiological and safety needs. The limbic, or emotional brain, overlays with the second and third layers: safety and needs for belonging and connection. Finally, the neocortex corresponds to the fourth and fifth layers: esteem and self-actualization.

I find this overlay helpful to understand where I'm acting from. Am I spending most of my time using my supercomputer prefrontal cortex, at even a fraction of its capability? Or am I stuck in my emotional center or in survival mode? If we want to become our Higher Selves, the part of our brain we need to leverage consistently becomes obvious. And that's why we need to make the bottom layers of our pyramid rock solid.

THE OVERLAP BETWEEN OUR LEVELS OF BEING AND THE NEEDS HIERARCHY

Let's look at this pyramid another way. We have four levels of being we operate from: physical, emotional, mental/intellectual, and spiritual. To live consciously and intentionally, we need to support and access all four levels.

The hierarchy of needs corresponds to our four levels of being. Physical being overlays with physiological and safety needs. Emotional being overlays with safety and belonging needs. Mental/intellectual being overlays with esteem and self-actualization needs. Spiritual being overlays with self-actualization.

This highlights the levels of our being that may be offline or unavailable in a particular scenario. Some examples to illustrate:

- If you are in immediate danger, are you focused on how it's making you feel and contemplating its causes and its greater meaning? Or are you focused on removing or neutralizing the threat and surviving? Once you're safe, that's when the emotions hit you. You'll mentally process after that, and eventually process it spiritually with more distance from the experience.
- If someone feels extraordinarily lonely and is looking for love, are they typically factoring in their longer-term intellectual and spiritual needs? Or are they more concerned with meeting their physical needs (like sex) and their emotional needs?
- When I was driving hard toward success and accomplishment before my wake-up call described in earlier chapters, I was operating from a mental and intellectual level, taking my emotional and physical needs being met for granted. Spirit was mostly shut out.

Much like Maslow's hierarchy, we will think, feel, and act from the level at or just above where we're solid. But remember, we can borrow our resources and strength from higher levels to solidify where we're weak. This is why tapping into our spirituality can help us mentally, emotionally, and physically. We talked about faith in Chapter 1 and its power. This illustrates how it can help make our lower levels whole. This is also the how behind *mind over matter*, as well as *feeling it to heal it*.

THE OVERLAP BETWEEN THE EMOTIONAL FREQUENCY SCALE, THE ENERGY CENTERS, AND THE NEEDS HIERARCHY

We're going even deeper. Remember the emotional frequency scale from the last chapter?

If certain emotions are frequently present or dominant, this can inform where we are strong, where we are weak, and subsequently where to begin. This will even direct you to where in your body you may want to focus. Look at Figure 12.2 and how the frequency scale overlaps with our bodies' energy centers, or chakras:

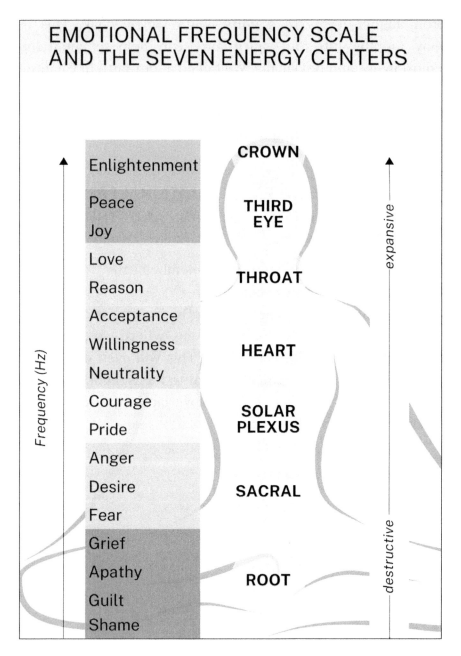

Figure 12.2: The emotional frequency scale and its correspondence to the body's seven energy centers, or chakras.

Every energy center has positive emotions and properties when in balance. Likewise, each has a shadow side when imbalanced. For instance, your root is grounding, your sacral is a source of creativity, and your solar plexus is a source of personal power. But if they're constricted or imbalanced, you may be unable to access their positive influence and instead feel the lower emotions on the scale.

If you've ever been to an energy healer, you're probably familiar with the concept of having energy stuck or imbalanced. If this is the first time you've heard that term, here's what it means in a nutshell. If you have unprocessed emotions (recall from the last chapter that emotion means *energy in motion*), that energy can get stuck in the body, creating a stagnation or imbalance. This can result from many things, like suppressing or denying feelings, holding onto grudges, or perhaps buried memories and their associated emotions. This is essentially a form of energetic constipation. We're meant to experience an emotion, process it, and release it. If we don't, we get energetically backed up and out of whack. When this happens, we can lose our connection to that energy center and feel cut off from its positive influence. Here's how blockage and imbalance can play out in real life:

- **Root:** Do you have deeply held guilt or shame? You may feel insecure or greedy, or withdraw from the physical world.
- **Sacral:** Have anger, desire, or fear you're not acknowledging or dealing with? It may show up as addiction, sexual dysfunction, or blocked creativity.
- **Solar Plexus:** Have feelings of arrogance or insecurity? It could present as issues around power (powerlessness or hoarding it) and control.

- **Heart:** Are you jealous, stubborn, in denial, or emotionally closed off? Relationship difficulties may be commonplace for you.
- **Throat:** Have difficulty speaking truth (which is love) or communicating effectively (reason)? It may show up as fear of speaking out, expressing yourself, or being dishonest.
- **Third Eye:** Restless, confused, or disconnected from your intuition? It may present as difficulty feeling happy or at peace.
- **Crown:** Disconnected from your purpose (and Spirit) or constantly wondering what the point of all the bullshit is in your life and the world? It can show up as cynicism and closed-mindedness.

In my experience, you can begin your healing in any area, leveraging strength and power from a healthy center, and direct it where it needs to go. For me, it's been a top-down approach, likely because my wake-up call was *heaven sent* from my grandparents. The dominant themes of my healing have been feeling (and physically becoming) lighter, more peaceful, joyful, expressive, and loving. (Of note, I've had several energy healers tell me my root and sacral are constricted. I guess I'm working my way down!) For others, you may be deeply healed from the bottom-up. Perhaps that comes from spending time in nature, grounding, or laying down roots in a place you can call home. The important thing is following the clues and your intuition on where to start.

Speaking of, here are a few more clues to follow.

ARE YOU OUT OF YOUR MIND?

There are other overlays with the hierarchy that have been demonstrative in pinpointing where I'm "thinking," feeling, and acting from. I say "thinking" with quotes because quite often, it's not our minds driving our thoughts, but rather, the body.

Until reading *Becoming Supernatural* by Dr. Joe Dispenza, it had never occurred to me that we often allow our body to *become* the mind. In other words, we let our bodies run the show. This happens over time as we become chemically addicted to specific emotions as if they were drugs. If unaware, we let our bodies run on autopilot in the endless pursuit of another hit from these chemical transmitters. Here's how this works, in Dr. Joe's words:

> Thoughts cause biochemical reactions in your brain that release chemical signals, and those chemical signals make the body feel exactly the way you were just thinking. Those feelings then cause you to generate more thoughts that make you feel the same way you were just thinking. So your thoughts drive your feelings, and your feelings drive your thoughts, and eventually this loop hardwires your brain into the same patterns, which conditions your body into the past. And because emotions are a record of past experiences, if you can't think greater than how you feel, this thinking–feeling loop keeps you anchored to your past and creates a constant state of being. This is how the body becomes the mind—or in time, how your thoughts run you and your feelings own you.[50]

At time of writing, I'd argue that most people are living in the past, in their body which has become their mind. But the Great Awakening is here. The more of us who make this conscious shift toward reclaiming our minds and aligning with Spirit, the more people we will wake up. Recall from Chapter 2 how a purse of pennies that doubles in value daily grows to over $5 million in thirty days. Our individual awakenings and growth compound and accelerate collective healing.

Part of awakening is gaining awareness of where the problem is. Going back to the energy centers discussed in the prior section and the areas you suspect are imbalanced, which part of you is correlated? Mind corresponds to Crown and Third Eye chakras; Heart (and Soul) to Throat and Heart chakras; Body to Solar Plexus, Sacral, and Root.

WHICH MIND ARE YOU IN (OR OUT OF)?

Here's the other part of this that I find mind-blowing. And yes, I love a good pun. The mind has three parts: subconscious, conscious, and superconscious.

Subconscious Mind: Also referred to as the unconscious mind, the subconscious is a vast reservoir of feelings, thoughts, urges, and memories outside our conscious awareness. It's responsible for automatic processes such as breathing, reflexes, and deeply ingrained habits and behaviors. The subconscious influences our beliefs, emotions, and motivations based on past experiences and learned behaviors.

Conscious Mind: This is the level of the mind aware of our surroundings and experiences. It's where rational thinking, decision-making, and reasoning occur. The conscious mind is involved in focused activities, logical thinking, and anything that requires direct attention and awareness.

Superconscious Mind: This level is often associated with higher consciousness and spirituality. It is considered the source of inspiration, intuition, universal consciousness, and a connection to the divine and infinite intelligence. The superconscious mind is the aspect of consciousness that transcends individual awareness, linking us to a greater wisdom and the entirety of existence. It's where we may experience profound insights, creativity, and a sense of unity with all life. (Remember the interconnectedness of minds in Chapter 9?)

The subconscious mind correlates to the body and the past. It aligns with material existence and the root, sacral, and solar plexus chakras. No coincidence these are tied to grounding. Conscious mind correlates to heart and soul through the heart and throat chakras. It is the bridge between the material world and spirit. The superconscious mind correlates to our mind when used as it was intended. This is our connection to divinity and Spirit. The third eye chakra overlaps conscious and superconscious. Corresponding to our pineal gland, think of it like the antenna that allows us to turn on the radio and tune into the station of the divine—and translate it into consciousness.

While creating this model, I considered a potential misalignment, given that heart and soul seem like they should correlate to the superconscious. But as we've discussed within these pages, perception is everything. If we shift our perspective to various ancient wisdom, the heart is indeed the seat of thought, will, and intention—or consciousness.[51] The Bible says, "Above all else, guard your heart, for everything you do flows from it."[52] The heart is the bridge between material existence (the body and lower chakras) and the divine (higher chakras and spirit).

THE MIND-BODY DISCONNECT

For many of us, our bodies and minds have disconnected from one another. We are either "in our heads" or overly focused on the physical world. We miss the synchronicities that abound around us when we're buried in thought or absorbed with our material, external surroundings. In either scenario, we are not in tune with the whispers of our somatic experience until the body has had enough and finally screams to be heard. The body correlates directly to our most basic needs. If we ignore these, our higher needs will not be met.

If the body's needs aren't met, the mind doesn't function optimally and can only focus on survival. Not on love, belonging, or self-esteem needs. As the Indian proverb goes, "A healthy person has many wishes, but an unhealthy person has only one." When you fall ill, you will do *anything* to be healthy again. You can focus on little (if anything) else when health has gone away.

Likewise, our soul cannot fulfill its mission if our minds are polluted and preoccupied with worries, fears, negativity, and perceived threats to our survival. Part of being present means caring for and being comfortable *in* our bodies, however they feel and whatever they look like.

PUTTING IT ALL TOGETHER

As the synthesis of these various paradigms came to me, I knew I needed to share it and make it applicable and accessible to inform an individual's unique starting point. Given how many perfectionists I work with (and knowing what it's like, since I'm unwinding that too), I'm hopeful this chapter has helped you get a better idea of where the fire is so you can go put it out instead of continuing to breathe in the smoke.

Here's a diagram in Figure 12.3 to put it all together. (You may want to bookmark this for future reference, or you can visit alessiacitro.com/book to download all the diagrams in this chapter.) To use this, choose a column where an aspect of yourself jumped out. Move your finger horizontally to see what correlates. This is a great way to see a holistic view of where you may want to start, as well as where you're strong and can leverage existing resources.

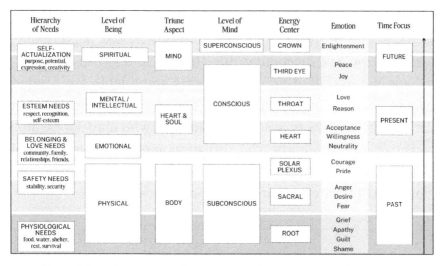

Figure 12.3 synthesizes everything from this chapter: the hierarchy of needs, levels of being, levels of mind, energy centers, and more.

COMING FULL CIRCLE ON WHY PURSUING SELF-ACTUALIZATION MATTERS

While writing this book, I learned about another level to Maslow's hierarchy. Community actualization would have been the sixth layer and pinnacle, inspired by his time living at Siksika, the Blackfoot reserve, in 1938.[53]

A potential shortcoming of Maslow's hierarchy as it stands today is the same problem responsible for much of the distress in Western culture: the emphasis on the individual with community and others as an afterthought. (Except, of course, how community can fill our need for love and belonging and, historically, safety.) With community actualization in its rightful place at the top of the hierarchy, we create the conditions as a community for individual needs to be met, paving the way for further expression of purpose among a greater number of people.

I've said it throughout, but *this* is why we pursue self-actualization and becoming our Higher Selves. *It's not about us*, and yet, *it's all about us*. Your gifts and talents are needed by another for them to thrive, just like you need others so you can thrive. And, there are those among us who may not be able to thrive independently. The rest of us rising to our potential helps ensure others don't get left behind. As I said before, the ripple you'll create by doing this work is far-reaching.

BE HER NOW EXERCISE:

Make notes of where you see areas of opportunity to improve and strengthen. What is one small change you can make today to create momentum and cultivate confidence?

Chapter 13

Thought, Word, and Deed

"Do not fight against pain; do not fight against irritation or jealousy. Embrace them with great tenderness, as though you were embracing a little baby. Your anger is yourself, and you should not be violent toward it. The only thing you have to do is to look after it with care, with love, with understanding, and with patience."

—Thich Nhat Hanh

DISCERNMENT: HOW TO RECOGNIZE AND CHOOSE YOUR HIGHEST THOUGHT, WORD, AND DEED

We have thousands of thoughts a day (6,000 to 70,000, depending on who you ask)—and up to 80 percent are negative and redundant![54] In this daily barrage of internal chatter, how can we identify the thoughts of our Higher Selves—those from a divine connection?

THOUGHT
Overcoming Negative Inner Dialogue

We touched on the importance of our thoughts and creating distance from Pam in Chapter 6; now, let's go deeper. While there are different approaches to bringing mindfulness to our thoughts, there is a universal commonality—to move into a state of observation, meaning you observe your thoughts, feelings, and actions from a distance without getting entangled in them. This is a key reason why embodying our Higher Self is so powerful. We're able to remove ourselves from our thoughts and experiences and view them through the lens of an observer—in this case, the best version of ourselves.

One of my best friends got really into yoga and meditation while we were in our twenties. Like me, Elisa has a brain that's always firing. Incredibly smart, she's always thinking about something. I'll never forget the way she described the benefits of the mindfulness she found through yoga, which I'll do my best to paraphrase here. She said, "Al, it's like my thoughts are a waterfall that I can now stand back and admire, whereas before, I was underneath the waterfall, getting pummeled by a never-ending onslaught." If you're under the waterfall right now, know that you, too, can begin the shift to observer.

One of the first things we must work toward is letting go of our resistance and judgment. We *all* think about weird shit! There's no point in denying or judging that—or resisting it. I believe in the adage that "what you resist persists." A way I have learned to shift my thoughts is to *allow* the ones I don't like. Allowing does not mean we participate in or endorse this negative internal dialogue. It means we allow the thought to come in. And then—we acknowledge it, so it stops vying for our attention. Anyone with children knows how effective acknowledging is when your kid is trying to command your attention. Ignore them, and they just get louder!

There are four steps to this process of observing and choosing a higher thought. To help you remember, use 4A:

- The first step is to become *aware* that we are not our thoughts but the thinkers of them.
- The next step is to *allow*. We don't need to resist our thinking because we have ultimate dominion over what happens in the six inches between our ears.
- The third step is to *acknowledge*. More on that in a moment.
- And finally, we choose and *affirm* a new, higher thought.

Let's use the example of the internal dialogue I've experienced writing this book to see how this works in action. For context, initially, this book *poured out of me* like water from a dam failure. And then, to say it was hard would be an understatement. Thoughts like, *What you're writing isn't any good. You don't seem inspired today. Maybe you should take a break (indefinitely)*, had been commonplace.

Before doing the inner work, I would've entertained these thoughts as my own. Or I would've fought them tooth and nail, getting frustrated and angry with myself in the process. Now, my reaction is different. I feel or hear the negative thought crop up. I allow it and listen with engagement—like you might to a child sharing a fantastical worry or concern. Then I internally reply with something like, *That's true, and you're right. The words aren't flowing today. But I committed to writing this book. How about this? I'll continue until the timer goes off, and then I can do something different if I want to. Besides, I might end up with a good idea, and at the very least, I'll feel good about keeping my word to myself.*

This is the process of mastering our thoughts. We become aware that we have the power to think whatever we choose, thanks to free will. Then, we allow the thought. We acknowledge it—which lowers the guard of the ego and Pam. And finally, we choose and affirm a *new, higher* thought. Rinse and repeat. Forever!

I invite you to do a bit of introspection here. How are you reacting now when negative or intrusive thoughts come up? Does that differ from the way you'd like to react? How can you apply love and compassion to yourself when intrusive or negative thoughts pop in? If these thoughts are part of our brain's mechanisms to keep us safe and alive, can you approach them with a level of gratitude for doing their job?

The deeper I get into this work, the more I approach my fragile ego like I would a scared child. When a child feels afraid, do you yell at them for it? Or do you reassure them, helping them regulate their emotions and ground back into safety? Imagining the fearful and negative voice as Pam or a very young version of me helps me oscillate between strength and compassion—and usually a combination of both.

The next time you go through the 4A method and choose a different thought—ask yourself, *what thought would my Higher Self choose?*

Thoughts are creative. Our feelings, words, actions, and realities all begin with thought. Will you wield this powerful tool to create a steel foundation on which to build the life you desire?

WORD

"Death and life are in the power of the tongue."

—Proverbs 18:21, *The Bible*, King James Version (KJV)

As someone who loves saying "bad" words, this section is what I, too, need to be reminded of. At the end of the day, I know my Higher Self says "fuck" when it's called for (and besides, how many other words serve as a noun, adjective, *and* verb?), but nevertheless, she probably doesn't swear like a sailor either. When I think of the best version of me and how she uses the spoken word, I imagine her being most vigilant to not speak negatively about herself, others, and circumstances. How does *your* Higher Self speak?

First, let's look at some of the ways in which language affects our lived experience.

Psycholinguistics

The words we use can affect our perceptions. Enter, the Sapir-Whorf Hypothesis. Also known as linguistic relativity, it suggests that the structure of language affects its speakers' cognition and worldview. Essentially, the language we use heavily influences how we think and perceive the world.

For example, language can affect our perception of time and space. Speakers might perceive time differently in languages like Mandarin, where there is a less distinct separation of past, present, and future tenses compared to English. This can influence how they plan for the future or reflect on the past by affecting their concept of time.[55]

In English, time is represented linearly and thought of horizontally. In Mandarin, time is represented linearly and *vertically.*[56] Here's how thoughts about saving money for a new car might compare. An English speaker might think about it with a clear timeline in mind, imagining the progression toward that goal as moving horizontally from left to right. For example, *I will save $200 a month for the next five years to buy a new car.* A Mandarin speaker might think about it like this: *Each $200 saved monthly elevates me one step closer to my goal, like climbing a staircase. Every month over these five years is a new level up, leading to the top where my new car awaits.* (Personally, I feel more empowered to think about my progress with elevation versus walking a long, flat road. I am adopting this sort of spatial thinking, and I invite you to join me!)

Language can affect color perception too. Russian speakers, who have different words for light blue (*goluboy*) and dark blue (*siniy*), can distinguish these shades more quickly than English speakers. This can affect perceptual experiences.[57]

Language can also affect how we experience emotions. Some languages have specific words for emotions that don't exist in other languages. For example, the Japanese word *amae* refers to a feeling of pleasurable dependence on another person. Having a specific word for this emotion could influence how individuals experience and express it.[58] Likewise, languages that use more embodied descriptions, like metaphors involving body parts to describe emotions (e.g., "a heavy heart"), might influence how individuals physically experience these emotions.[59]

While you can't change where you were born or your native language, I share the above to lay the foundation for how our words and language affect our perceptions and thus our realities. Now let's dive into using language for your highest good.

The Mind–Body Connection

If we're to fulfill our Higher Selves' missions, remaining in good health is a sacred imperative. What you listen to and believe influences your physical health and well-being. Many studies support this, including a Harvard study of hotel housekeepers.[60]

In the 2007 study, none of the eighty-four hotel housekeepers participating knew that the physical work they performed on the job was considered exercise, nor that it surpassed the US Surgeon General's recommendation of thirty minutes of exercise per day. 66.6 percent of the housekeepers said they did not exercise regularly, and 36.8 percent said they did not exercise at all. The researchers split the housekeepers into an informed group and a control group. The informed group was told the physical movement of their jobs exceeded the surgeon general's exercise recommendations and how many calories they burned through various tasks. The control group was not given any of this information. (The housekeepers in the study were from seven different hotels, each of which had participants only from the informed group or the control group. This ensured an informed participant wouldn't unknowingly share this information and skew the data.)

Learning this information changed the informed group's perceptions. They perceived themselves as getting more exercise. Their workload and level of exercise outside of work did not change. This simple shift in perception changed them on a physical level. The informed group lost an average of two pounds, their systolic blood pressure decreased by ten points, and there were significant improvements in body fat percentage, BMI, and waist-to-hip ratio. Meanwhile, the control group saw no significant changes.

Are you beginning to see why I'm so intent on informing *you* of how capable and powerful you are? If you believe what you're reading (thus all the citations and data!), it will change your perception. And a change in perception can affect changes in our reality by changing our beliefs, thoughts, emotions, actions, habits, and thus, our lives and destinies.

Beware that this goes both ways, though. A 2006 Canadian study investigated how women's math performance could be influenced by their beliefs about gender differences in math ability.[61] Female participants were exposed to fake research reports before taking a math test. These reports suggested that men were better than women at math, but for different reasons: One report attributed the difference to genetic factors, while another attributed it to experiential factors. (There were other fake reports without this information that served as controls.) The study aimed to see how these different explanations affected the women's performance on the math test.

You can guess what the researchers found. The women who read reports stating that men are better in math due to genetic advantages did significantly worse on the test than those who were given the reports stating that any advantage men had was due to experiential factors.

This study highlights two key things. One, perceiving you're disadvantaged or not as good as someone else can lead you to perform as such. This creates a fixed mindset—that we are the way we are, without the agency to improve. Two, thinking you're disadvantaged due to a lack of experience does not negatively impact performance. This highlights the power of a growth mindset. Your capability is undiminished if you believe a gap exists purely because you haven't "gotten in the reps" yet.

Likewise, shifting to an optimistic outlook and verbally affirming that perspective helps to manage stress and keep it from escalating into a chronic state of being. Optimism is not about being "Pollyanna" and unrealistic. It's an actual means of improving our resilience in the face of adversity and helps drive success.[62] The beauty of this is it creates a positive feedback loop. The better you feel, the more positive you are—in thought *and* word.

Words Are Creative

Creation narratives across many cultures and religious traditions share a common thread: that the world was spoken into existence. The ancient Hindu scripture, The Rigveda, states that the world was created from the sound "om," and that this sound is the vibration from which the entire universe emanates. Norse mythology is similar, with the primordial void being filled with the sounds of the first being, from which all the elements of the world eventually emerge. The Māori believe the world started in a state of nothingness or darkness and that light came in through the incantations and chants of the gods. The New Testament begins with the Gospel of John (1:1): "In the beginning, was the Word, and the Word was with God, and the Word was God." In ancient Egypt, the world was created through the heart and tongue (thought and speech) of the god Ptah. In Judaism, God is Yahweh, which means *I am*. Is it any wonder why these two words and whatever follows them are so powerful?

People all over the world use spoken prayers and chants to connect with the divine and to manifest changes. Perhaps I missed a calling as an anthropologist, but I find it fascinating how many diverse traditions and cultures have similar creation stories and myths passed down over thousands of years. Another nudge that we all have more in common than not.

In the last chapter, we discussed the body's energy centers, or chakras. Interestingly, the sacral and throat are the two chakras with the power to create. The sacral chakra creates using the physical and material. The throat creates by *speaking*. We vocalize thoughts, ideas, and intentions into existence.

If words are creative, what are we speaking into existence? How are we speaking about ourselves, others, and our circumstances?

Masaru Emoto conducted experiments exposing water to various stimuli, including positive and negative words.[63] Water that was exposed to positive messages (like love and gratitude), harmonious music, and beneficial conditions created beautifully structured and symmetrical ice crystals. Water exposed to negative influences formed disfigured crystals or none at all. Some of the negative messages the water was exposed to included phrases like, "You fool," "You make me sick," and "I will kill you." What are the emotional frequencies of these messages? Shame, fear, and death, some of the lowest on the scale. We're made up of about 60 percent water.[64] Imagine how negative words might affect us on a biological level.

It's so common to say things like "*I'm dying* to visit Europe," "*I'd kill* for abs like that," or "*I'm dead*" when something is funny. And look, I do this too—it's how we often talk. But are we speaking life over ourselves? Or death? Another example: "I can't wait" instead of "I'm looking forward." I struggle with patience as is without speaking it into existence even more so! *Looking forward* feels better.

My dad espouses a lot of wisdom from his Sicilian upbringing, and he always quotes my grandfather: "Be immaculate with your word." This also happens to be one of Don Miguel Ruiz's *Four Agreements*. To be immaculate with your word means to speak with integrity. To choose our words carefully. To not speak against ourselves or to gossip about others. Easier said than done, but like anything done with intention and grace, it's a habit we can build and strengthen.

I once heard a three-part criteria by which to test everything before it leaves our lips: *Is it true? Is it kind? Is it necessary?*

DEED

Manifestation has gone mainstream, but it's largely misunderstood or misinterpreted. You can create all the vision boards, say all the affirmations, and do all the visualizations, but if you stop short of acting ... spoiler alert: nothing happens. Action is the magic ingredient, and it need not feel like work.

There is a Zen paradigm that feels meant for us ideators: "Stop thinking and talking about it and there is nothing you will not be able to know." If you also love to overthink and verbally process, I see you. But we can't forget to integrate and execute.

Remember, action isn't so much about *doing* as it is about *being*. When we are *being* in accordance with the best version of ourselves, action happens with much more ease. It doesn't need to be forced. It doesn't need to be arduous. It doesn't need to be perfect. (And yes, that means you can stop procrastinating, since that's perfectionism in another form.)

If you feel regret over actions you didn't take or opportunities and experiences that passed you by, take heart.

One of my very favorite and most recited mantras is, "Nothing meant for me gets away." Even if you disagree, what if you could reframe those "misses" into steppingstones and teaching moments that got you where you are *now*? Nothing happens in a vacuum. That missed experience or opportunity set the stage for what came your way instead.

Perhaps what I love most about thinking, speaking, and acting in accordance with my Higher Self is that every time I do, *I am her*. Like we discussed in Chapter 9 on the quantum, that's the powerful truth about being her now. We can access this version of us whenever we decide to. And *now* is all there is.

BE HER NOW EXERCISE:

For the next week, be more aware of your thoughts, words, and deeds. Are these reflective of the authentic you who is channeling her Higher Self? If not, with love and grace, ask yourself how you can think, speak, and act in alignment with her. We won't always get it right, but with practice comes progress.

Chapter 14
Outward Embodiment

"The body is not an apology. It is not something to be fixed, hidden, or neglected. It is something to be celebrated, honored, and occupied fully."

—Sonya Renee Taylor

Being true to your Higher Self and bringing her into existence hinges on embodying her. In Chapter 11, we discussed energetics and emotional embodiment, which is the internal half of the equation. Now, let's discuss why we must work to embody her outwardly and how we can.

SHOWING UP AS HER

How we show up in the world—and how we feel about the way we show up—either contracts or expands us. We are closed off while contracted. Openness and expansiveness are where we attract what's meant for us. It is in this state of expansion that miracles happen. It is a priority to outwardly embody our Higher Self because when we take on her energy, we summon what she calls in.

Let's make this tangible with an experience we've all had. Think of a time when you knew you didn't look your best, and you *felt* it. That energy likely preceded you. It's the difference between how you feel on a rushed morning when you're in the school drop-off line in your pajamas versus those days when you feel put together.

As I wrote this book, I received a serendipitous message from a personal stylist I'm connected to, Danielle King. She introduced me to a term I found important enough to share with you here: *enclothed cognition.*

Enclothed cognition is defined as the psychological phenomenon where the clothes a person wears significantly affect their psychological processes, including their attitudes, behaviors, and performance. This concept suggests that our attire can influence not only how we are perceived by others but also how we perceive ourselves and our abilities.[65] (And you remember how important perception is from the Harvard study of hotel housekeepers in the last chapter!)

What Danielle shared with me is powerful:

> Your clothes are not just fabric on hangers you can buy in the store. They're *mood managers.* If you've ever thrown something on and suddenly felt on top of the world, you know what I'm talking about. That's the real deal—*enclothed cognition.* It's like your wardrobe has this secret power to amp up your vibe and shift your attitude. By selecting garments that resonate with our desired mindset, we tap into the profound connection between attire and attitude, experiencing a genuine shift in how we perceive ourselves and interact with the world. Dressing as our Higher Selves ensures that the

outside matches our incredible inside. Dress better. Feel better. Do better. [66]

Drop the mic, Danielle. And whether we like it or not, we know she's right.

This isn't about dressing to the nines every day. It's about how we *feel*. You know those days when your look is on point? You love how your skin or makeup looks, you're having a great hair day, you're wearing an outfit you love, etc.? I don't know about you, but I feel *so good* on those days.

Now, have you ever kept yourself from looking (and feeling) that good because you thought it might look like you were "trying too hard?" Or have you ever had the thought that it's superficial because people should love you for who you are inside?

Both were recurrent and dominant thoughts of mine for years. If you can relate, I've got a loving reminder. These are clever tricks the ego plays to keep us "safe," small, and unseen. (Yes, that's Pam back on her bullshit, again.) While it's true that what's inside us matters most, it's a fact that our outward presentation and energy determine whether someone will want to get to know us in a deeper and more meaningful way. It's why companies invest in branding and marketing. You can have an incredible product, but without the presentation and packaging to match, it may not have the impact it deserves. Outwardly embodying our Higher Selves and exuding that energy helps us connect with those we're meant to serve and thus fulfill our mission.

What if shifting to spaciousness and confidence centers on mindfulness and intention? There's a Buddhist concept around this, exemplified by putting on perfume or cologne.

Mindfully putting on perfume makes you more aware of how you present yourself. Ultimately, the intention is to connect. If fragrance isn't your thing, what can you bring to interactions—either physically or energetically—to connect with others more deeply?

Since I began exploring and experimenting with these questions, I've felt a shift energetically and have had more fun with my personal style. This practice of mindful intention has brought out playfulness and a spark that had been shelved.

There are still days when I run an errand, and I look and feel like Oscar the Grouch. But often, I'm showing up in the energy and confidence of my Higher Self. What a difference it makes inside—and out.

JOYFUL MOVEMENT

I'm not a person who needs to move my body or work out for my sanity. I can take it or leave it. But my energy is notably different on the days I make it happen. There's more of it, and it's higher vibe.

This is not a call to tell you to hit the gym. If that's your thing, cool, but there are plenty of other ways to move and get your energy flowing. Is it dancing in your office while you take a break between projects? Is it doing cartwheels on the lawn with your kiddo? (My personal favorite!) Is it taking a ten-minute gratitude walk outside? Or perhaps doing squats in the kitchen while your coffee brews? This gets to be fun and fit into our lives however we choose.

I was born in 1985, and I have so many memories of the toxic diet culture that permeated American life all through my childhood and coming of age. If you're a millennial, you might share many of these associations between movement and dieting. Perhaps you bristle at working out because it's associated with punishing your body. I regularly feel this resistance, even though I enjoy exercise when I do it. Becoming aware of this and being able to name it has helped me create distance between these automatic associations and the truth. What I know is true for me is that it feels good to move. It feels good to sweat, stretch, and get stronger. It feels good to play, climb, and run! It also feels good to rest and relax. Make sure you do the latter too.

Sometimes I think about how much I take mobility for granted and how much easier my life is because I'm able-bodied. Becoming aware of privilege is important. When we moved into our first home, our neighbor across the street used a wheelchair due to aggressive brain cancer that quickly ravaged his body and took his life. He'd been an athlete before he got sick. During that time, I remember being diligent about working out because I was regularly reminded of how fortunate I was to be *able* to.

Isn't that true of so many things in life? We say we "have to" or we "should," but really, we *get to*. I hope that one day, I'll develop a gratitude muscle so strong that I no longer need that reminder.

Embodying your Higher Self ultimately comes down to one thing. Honoring *you*. The person you were created to be can't shine if we don't give her the chance. Disease, immobility, and self-loathing all dim her light. We choose to physically embody our Higher Selves because we love and accept ourselves enough to do so. We don't do it to meet societal expectations, or for shallow and superficial reasons. We do it to feel good and radiate. Because energy is everything, and the more we shine, the more we heal, and the more we fulfill our soul's calling, the more we make waves that can heal the world.

BE HER NOW REFLECTION:

- What would it look like to outwardly embody your Higher Self in a way that feels good to you?
- What would it look like to move your body on a more regular basis, to access more and better energy, and to cultivate creativity and joy?
- Write down some ideas and put *one* into practice for the next week. Make this change small. Remember, we're shifting from grandiose to granular. Rate how you feel today and compare it to how you feel at the end of the week. Reassess from there.

As you contemplate what it would feel like to move and show up as your Higher Self, consider how this would help you reconnect to your body. If your body is whispering or screaming its needs to you, how could mindful intention help so you can be, do, and have more?

Because this is part of the audit stage, consider what to stop, start, and continue in these areas. You can begin a list, or if you haven't yet, head to alessiacitro.com/book for a workbook to help you organize your thoughts.

Chapter 15

Inputs Determine Outputs

"The mind is not a vessel to be filled, but a fire to be kindled."

—Plutarch

Now that you are aware, aligned, and have a deep understanding of your needs and where to begin meeting them, let's look at your inputs. What are you consuming and being exposed to, and how are you being affected? This chapter provides some areas to consider before we move on to designing habits in Part Four: Activate, which immediately follows this chapter.

Below is a series of questions that will further inform where to place your initial focus. Answer these honestly and without judging yourself. In case you need to hear this, I'd like to remind you: you're reading a book called *Higher Self Habits*—and that fact alone means you're doing the work and are farther along than you think you are. Also, note the questions you're saying yes to, especially at the higher levels of the hierarchy. Those are your well-resourced areas that can help you strengthen the others.

You can download a free digital version of the assessment below at alessiacitro.com/book.

HIERARCHY OF NEEDS SELF-ASSESSMENT
Basic Needs

- Do you have shelter?
- Are you able to access clean and safe drinking water easily?
- Are you adequately hydrated?
- Are you eating enough each day?
- Are you eating food that gives you energy? Or are you eating food that depletes your energy? (And while I love coffee, I'm not referring to the energy you get from a Red Bull, a double espresso, or a sugary drink like Mountain Dew.)
- Are you getting enough sleep?
- Do you have clothing necessary for the climate you live in?
- Do you have access to basic healthcare and medical services?

Safety and Stability Needs

- Is your home safe?
- Is your neighborhood safe?
- Is your state or country safe?
- Do you have a baseline of financial stability? (e.g., you can pay your bills, you have enough money for food, you can handle an emergency that pops up that costs $1,000 or less.)
- Are you prepared for potential emergencies costing $1,000 or more?
- Are you healthy? Or is your physical or mental health a concern?

- Is your life feeling stable in general? (e.g., you have a functional relationship (if you're in one); a stable job; you feel generally even-keeled.)
- Are you satisfied with your current living situation?
- Do you have a reliable mode of transportation if needed?

Emotional and Belonging Needs

- Do you have a friend you can count on and trust? (More than one is gravy.)
- Do you have social or community groups you're part of? If not, are there some you can plug into?
- If you're in a romantic relationship, is it fulfilling, supportive, and healthy?
- Do you have family you can count on and that you love?
- Do you feel like you're part of a team at work? If you're an entrepreneur and work alone, do you have entrepreneurial friends you can co-work and collaborate with when needed?
- Do you feel emotionally supported by your friends and loved ones?
- Are you able to express your emotions freely and honestly in your relationships?

Self-Esteem Needs

- Do others respect you?
- Do you respect yourself?
- Are you recognized for your contributions and accomplishments?
- Do you feel capable, in general?

- Do you feel you have the freedom and independence to live how you wish?
- Are you setting and achieving personal goals?
- Are you maintaining a balance in your life that you feel good about?
- Do you feel confident in your ability to make decisions and navigate life's challenges?

Self-Actualization Needs

- Are you actively pursuing your passions and interests?
- Are you actively involved in any hobbies or activities that bring you joy?
- Do you have opportunities for learning and personal development?
- Are you engaged in activities that challenge and inspire you?
- Do you have a sense of purpose and direction in your life?
- Are you making a positive impact on others or your community?

So, how did it go? Where on the hierarchy do you need to start? What do you most *want* to change? What's the easy, low-hanging fruit? Quick wins pay dividends upfront and later. These are where we start.

And if you're feeling like you've got a lot of ground to cover, let's acknowledge that and know that it's okay—and let's reframe. A habit of mine is putting everything possible in context, so let's quickly do that here. If you answered "yes" to having shelter, congratulations. You're in the 80 percent of the world's population that's fortunate enough to have a roof over their heads.[67] If you have access to clean drinking water, congratulations again. 10 percent of the world does not.[68]

You may feel like you have quite a few holes in your boat that need patching, but you're doing much better and are more well-resourced than you realize. And remember, if you're strong in areas higher up the hierarchy, you can use those resources to help fill the gaps below.

Let's look at some other inputs that are a bit more nuanced.

WHAT DO YOU CONSUME?

When we hear the word "consume," our minds usually go to food or drink. And yes, eating nutrient-rich food as often as we can is important. So is not drinking to excess, smoking, or doing hard drugs. But you already know all that. I'm a lot more interested in what your *mind* is consuming.

According to Literacy, Inc., 33 percent of US high school graduates never read another book after high school.[69] And here you are, about to finish a personal development book that covers neuroscience, the quantum, and more. You're doing well, my friend. Consider the below forms of consumption, too.

Social Media

Like any tool, social media can be used to our benefit or detriment. As of writing in March 2024, internet users across the world spend an average of two hours and thirty-one minutes on social media *each day*.[70] This equates to thirty-eight days spent on social media every year. For context, can you imagine being on social media with no break from Thanksgiving to New Year's Day? Think of missing the entire holiday season and what really matters to us because of the tiny screens in our hands. Puts it into perspective, doesn't it?

Before you go deleting all your apps, approach this with curiosity. Are you using social media to escape? As a business tool? Both? When you use it, do you find yourself buying stuff you don't need? Does social media make you feel better or worse, generally? One of my coaching clients shared something in my group program I'll never forget. Consumers of apps and drugs are both referred to as *users*. Are you using social media, or is it using you? Let these answers point you toward more intentional usage and time spent.

What about the people you follow online? If their vacations, beautiful homes, and appearance make you feel like shit about your own life, get curious about why that is. If you feel envy, that's a clue you desire these things. No judgment, just facts: you would be better served spending time creating these circumstances in your own life and less time watching others live it. If an account makes you feel icky, unfollow. Remember, the algorithm on all social platforms works the same way as your brain's RAS that we discussed in Chapter 5. Tell it what you think is important (and what's not) and begin to filter out the noise. Curate an online experience that supports your growth and optimal mental and emotional states. I try to do a purge of accounts a few times a year and I immediately unfollow anything that makes me feel sad, anxious, or inadequate.

If you get sucked in for hours at a time, you can use time limits within the apps or in your phone's settings. Monitoring my screen time report has also helped me be more mindful. I still buy plenty of crap I don't need because those ads just *know me*, but hey, progress over perfection.

Other Media

There is a time and place for most everything. When you read the following, consider your *habits* as they relate to media and whether they're working for or against you.

What TV and movies do you watch? Are they dark and disturbing, or funny and lighthearted? Do you generally watch to learn and grow? Or to be entertained and escape? Do you feel uplifted and empowered by what you watch? Or sad, anxious, and powerless? Does what you watch expand your mind, or does it reinforce existing beliefs and views? Do you feel like you wasted an hour of your life when you're done?

What about what you listen to? If it's music, does it evoke good feelings or make you want to dance? I'm sure most of you reading this have donated your Limp Bizkit and Papa Roach CDs from high school by now, but if you still listen to angry music on the regular, how's that working for you?

How about podcasts and radio? Are you listening to pundits pop off on politics or to a podcast with reality TV stars rehashing fabricated drama? Or are you listening to hosts and information that empower, uplift, and inspire you?

Something I've never been able to unhear is why radio, movies, and TV shows are referred to as *programming*. The name says it all. Whatever you watch and listen to will program you if you unconsciously consume it. It'll also change your emotional state. Watching negative news has been found to increase negative emotions,[71] and starting your day with a mere three minutes of negative news in the morning increases your chance of having a bad day by 27 percent![72] If you have a habit of turning on the news first thing in the morning, this might be one to consider stopping.

PRIME TIME

If watching negative news in the morning is 27 percent more likely to make you have a bad day, it's probably not just the content of the news but how it's *priming* you. How we begin anything matters because it influences what follows and, thus, the result. So, how are you starting your day?

There are many wonderful books about the importance of morning routines that you can find in the suggested reading list and at alessiacitro.com/book, so I'll keep this short. Consider your typical morning and how you can make it more supportive in becoming your Higher Self. Some ideas to get your wheels turning:

- Are you waking up later than you want to, feeling frantic and rushed?
- Do you have quiet, intentional, introspective time before your day gets started? (Journaling, meditation, stretching, and reading are some ways to do so.)
- Do you close open loops from the day before? Our brains *love* completing cycles. This might look like making the bed or unloading the dishwasher.
- Do you begin your day with gratitude and excitement? Or do you feel more like Bill Murray in the classic movie *Groundhog Day*?

If you're a night owl, you may balk at the morning routine talk but know you can make it work for you. I was never a morning person and had issues at both work and school because of it. (I might've gotten good grades and been a stellar leader in student government, but that didn't stop my high school from putting me on a well-deserved attendance contract for being late so many times!) Now I happily get up at 5 a.m. most days.

There's hope for the rest of you night owls too. This is not to say you need to wake up that early, but to reassure you that you can change—if you want to.

Three quick tips on getting up early, if you want to:

1. Get a sunrise alarm clock. The gradual brightening of the light will gently wake you by triggering the receptors in your eyes that signal to your body it's morning and time to produce the cortisol that helps you wake up energized.
2. Put a second alarm clock away from your bed where you have to physically get up to turn it off. (I still rely on this and suspect I always will!)
3. Have a cup of hot lemon water first thing in the morning. It'll lock in early waking as a pleasurable sensory experience, and you'll start to crave it. Sounds weird, but it works!

If any of the above sound interesting to implement, I'll give you the behavior design framework to put them into practice very soon.

A final note on priming. If mornings are difficult, look at what's happening the night before. Great mornings start with great evenings. Some questions to consider:

- If you're going to bed late, why? Can you solve for the reason if there is one? Can you move your bedtime up by fifteen minutes until you reach your desired time?
- Are you closing loops you opened earlier that day? For example, is your kitchen or house a mess when you go to bed, and that dread and anxiety is carrying over to the morning?

- Are you eating dinner or having coffee too late and it's affecting your sleep? (Alcohol is a common culprit for shitty sleep too, and one most people don't realize.)
- Are you on your phone, computer, or watching TV before bed, and the blue light is potentially affecting your sleep?

Most problems are multifactorial, but looking at your habits holistically may provide insights into why certain issues persist. More on that in the next chapter.

RELATIONSHIPS

Like anything in life, people are paradoxical. We are social creatures who require other people to function. At the same time, other people can do great harm or hold us back, making us dysfunctional. Being as selective as possible with the people we surround ourselves with is one of the most important exercises in self-love.

If you know you're surrounded by people who are not contributing to your elevation and evolution, what can you do to minimize your exposure and begin meeting people who will? Is it intentionally attending events with like-minded people? Is it finding meetups with people who have shared interests? Is it moving to a new neighborhood, town, state, or country? (Moving to Scottsdale, Arizona, totally helped me grow as a person and budding entrepreneur, but there were many wonderful people where we moved from too. Proximity to action and events helps, but it's also important to not use where we live as an excuse. There are great people everywhere!) I know it's not always easy making new friends as an adult, but your Higher Self is counting on you to try.

We've all heard the famous Jim Rohn quote that we are the average of the five people we spend the most time with. Do everything within your resources and power to get in rooms and environments with people you admire. Proximity is powerful.

Some of the hardest lessons I've had to learn have been around boundaries and expectations as they relate to relationships. For example, one of the most difficult aspects of personal development is outgrowing people you love and care about. I have yet to meet a person I admire who hasn't encountered this. This has been my litmus test for whether to continue a relationship:

- Is maintaining this relationship hurting or helping me? (Other ways to ask this: Does this relationship drain or energize me? Do I feel better or worse after interacting with this person?)
- What does my inner knowing say when I ask if this relationship is for a reason, a season, or a lifetime? If for a reason or a season, has it run its course and now it's time to let it go in gratitude?
- What is the relationship based on, and am I expecting something unreasonable? (For instance, are you expecting your childhood best friend with a very different life to understand—and get excited about— your latest business endeavor?)
- To continue this relationship in a mutually beneficial way, what do I need to change in terms of expectations and perceptions? Are boundaries required on either end? Do we need to have a conversation to level-set or clear the air?

- Is this relationship strained because it began when I was *not* my authentic self, and now that I'm moving into my truth, it's misaligned?

When I really went deep on this personal growth stuff, some of my most treasured relationships suffered. We can get really excited about who we're becoming and it's deflating when people we love don't share our enthusiasm. Here I'd offer this: Unless they are actively trying to discourage or keep you down, don't make it mean anything. We all grow and evolve at different rates, walking our own unique paths. You cannot expect your friends to share your frame of reference and all your interests. You may feel judged when they don't want to come along for the ride or hear the play by play, but you're judging them for not wanting to! Or perhaps you're expecting relationships to function like Swiss Army knives, able to adapt to your every need and evolution. That's not realistic or fair. Once I realized this, strained relationships became great again. (Of course, I was the one who'd caused the strain to begin with, and shifting my perceptions and expectations healed it. Acknowledging this and apologizing if necessary doesn't hurt either.)

BE HER NOW REFLECTIONS:

- Have you been holding those you love to unreasonable expectations based on the foundation of your relationship? For example, do you have a best friend who hasn't been enthusiastic about your growth or business, but who you know would move mountains to be there for you and your family if you ever needed them? Likewise, are you wishing your professional relationships were more personally supportive? There will be unicorn relationships that span across both, but most of the time, roles are more defined. These aren't personal shortcomings, that's just life.

- Which relationships can you feel more gratitude for?
- Which relationships need expectation or perception adjustments?
- Which need boundaries?
- Which need to be let go?

Now that you've completed the audit phase, where do you see your starting point? What are the lowest points in your needs hierarchy that need to be solidified? Where are you absolutely crushing it that can help you downstream? What's misaligned that needs to go?

As we leave the audit stage, take a moment to give yourself a hug, high five, or whatever feels good. You are absolutely crushing it by continuing this process of uncovering. Now, the rubber meets the road, and we begin to put it into practice.

Part Four: Activate

"Words may inspire, but only action creates change."

—Simon Sinek

Chapter 16

Domino Habits

"Every small action ignites a reaction. Like dominoes in a line, what we do today propels what happens tomorrow. Be the domino that falls toward positive change."

—Unknown

You are now intimately aware of the areas in your life you want to improve and the ones you're solid in. You have a well-informed idea of where to start and why. With this awareness, you can begin finding and lining up your dominoes for transformation.

As I began making big changes in my life, I inadvertently leveraged what I call *domino habits*. This concept effectively created a shortcut because it helped me do more with less.

I used the following process to inform where to start with changes. It began with a two-part question:

1. If I zoom out, what behaviors create the most disruption in my life and bleed into multiple areas?

2. Of those, what is the easiest and most impactful place to start? (This is where your answers to the previous assessment come in handy too.)

I looked objectively at the various parts of my life that were problematic. Pulling back the curtain entirely, here's what I saw: drinking to inebriation several nights a week, impulsive online spending (almost exclusively at night, while drinking), lack of patience, weight gain, low energy, a hard time getting out of bed in the morning, overwhelm, the feeling of being on a hamster wheel, brain fog, marital strain, and a lack of presence.

Then, I looked for the throughline in the form of a *domino habit*. Did these problems have a common denominator, even to a small degree? The answer stared me in the face. It was alcohol.

If you've ever set up and knocked down dominoes, you know how this works.

FINDING THE LEADING DOMINO

Alcohol was the domino that started a cascade of negativity throughout my life. It contributed to every single other feeling, behavior, or circumstance that was a problem. I also realized this one behavior of drinking to excess had created its own cycle and feedback loop. Maybe drinking isn't your escape or anesthetic of choice, but perhaps you can relate. You feel a difficult emotion, you numb it (with food, booze, drugs, porn, shopping, sex, reality TV, etc.), you feel shame for numbing it (and how you numbed it), so you do another numbing behavior to escape feeling shame, and on and on it goes.

Now, I am *not* qualified to coach you on overcoming addiction. If your problematic behaviors are "bad habits," read on. But if you have even a slight inkling that it's a dependency or addiction, seek professional help that can provide you with effective support, tools, and resources. (You can find a list to help you get started in the Appendix.)

When you consider the areas in your own life that need improvement, can you find a common denominator or throughline that leads to your domino habit? If the throughline is a big or painful one, like realizing you have an addiction or compulsion of some kind, you may not be able to see it, and that's okay too. I may be an outlier in that I was able to see this for myself without the help of a counselor or therapist.

That said, many times the throughline may seem insignificant or innocuous. Or it may be so deeply ingrained or a lifelong behavior that you don't know any different. Both are reasons people sometimes can't see the throughline themselves. This is where a great therapist, coach, or counselor can come in clutch.

Here's a relatable example. Maybe your domino habit is eating sugary processed snacks. You don't eat nearly enough protein (which can result in sugar cravings). You have energy crashes, irritability, and weight you can't seem to shed. This has caused mood swings and low libido, which have led to relationship strain with your partner. Your self-confidence has taken a hit too, which keeps you from sharing your gifts and talents. It affects your professional performance, as well as your fulfillment and income.

If processed sugar-laden snacks are the domino, what is causing you to eat them? Perhaps it's the only thing that's quick and easy to eat during the day. If that's the case, can removing them solve the problems downstream? Maybe, and maybe not. This process is trial and error. A good starting point could be stocking healthy, nutrient-dense grab-and-go type snacks, then noting how this *one* change begins to affect the other behaviors.

When we zero in on a domino habit, we'll likely need to swap in a desired habit instead. In this example, that might be regular grocery shopping, meal prep, or stocking ingredients for a protein smoothie you can make in a few minutes. If we give this solution the time required to note changes that occur and we don't swap this "bad" domino habit for another detrimental one, we can solve the downstream problems with much less effort. (We'll go deep on stopping unwanted habits in Chapter 19, but I want to get your wheels turning.)

Other times, it may not be clear what the domino habit is because it's entangled. For example, let's say you have low energy that's keeping you from doing the things you need or want to accomplish. You've taken inventory of your life and you've found a few areas that aren't optimal. You don't get enough sleep. You aren't exercising or moving your body regularly. You struggle to wake up on time. You aren't drinking enough water. What's the domino habit?

The answer is it depends. They're all interrelated, and it's a bit of chicken and egg—which comes first? Two questions to ask yourself here, with discernment. First, which of these do you know or suspect is having the biggest impact? Second, is there one that would resolve the rest if rectified? If you're not sure, where do you want to begin experimenting? I think back to learning about variables in math and science class. You can only change one at a time to pinpoint which variable affects the rest and to what degree. Approach entangled habits the same way. Start with the one that feels easiest and that you're most interested in changing.

Continuing with the last example on low energy, what if you're just dehydrated? This is why referencing the hierarchy of needs is helpful. Hydration is at the base of the hierarchy. It plays into body temperature regulation, prevents dry mouth that can wake you up, and creates better sleep quality. So, if you drink more water, you might sleep better. And if you sleep better, you might wake up on time and exercise. And you always feel energized after a workout. So, drinking more water for proper hydration may be the domino habit to focus on.

Let's expand on this further so you can see the process. If you focus on creating a hydration habit, what is making it hard to drink water now? What can you do to make it easier? Perhaps it's getting a water bottle you take everywhere. Or putting a hydration supplement in your water to make it taste better, which has the dual benefit of making it more appealing *and* hydrating you more effectively. (I realize most scenarios aren't this simple, but this approach is universal. We will get more complex in Chapters 17 and 18.)

DOMINO HABITS CAN BE POSITIVE

Perhaps your domino habit is getting up thirty minutes earlier than your children, so you have time to read, meditate, and drink coffee in silence. (As a mom, I enjoy coffee most when it's hot and I'm alone!) The time to yourself enables you to start your day calmly. You feel more patient and prepared. This carries into the rest of the day, and at bedtime, you realize your whole day went better. Waking up a bit earlier is a positive domino habit. And yes, this example is from personal experience!

Now it's time to learn everything you'll need about behavior design and how to find the right behaviors to create a desired habit.

BE HER NOW REFLECTION:

What is a domino habit you want to stop and swap for a supportive one? Is there one you want to create that could move the needle in multiple areas with little to no effort? Keep your answers handy—you'll design for these behaviors next!

Chapter 17

Build on Steel with Behavioral Science Basics

"We first make our habits, then our habits make us."

—John Dryden

What is the secret sauce to crafting habits that last? Simplicity and leaning into what you *already want to do* while tapping into the reward center of your brain.

If you have struggled to create lasting habits, it's not your fault. Seriously. It's not due to weakness, a lack of willpower, or a character flaw. *You've simply had behavior design flaws that you didn't have the tools to analyze and correct.* That changes right now. And it's simpler (and more fun!) than you think.

In fact, behavior design is so simple that I'm devoting a comparatively small section of this book to the *how*. As you read the final part of this book, remember that the real work is in the mindset and energetics we've covered and done upfront (and get to keep doing!). What follows here is the "easy" part.

These next chapters contain critical concepts that you'll want to refer back to for as long as it takes to encode them in your memory. I highly encourage you to mark up this final part of the book with notes and a highlighter. If you're so inclined, add sticky tabs, take notes in a notebook, the companion workbook, or on your phone, or use whatever system works for you. But please, commit to imprinting this in your memory and making it easy to return to when needed. Speaking from experience, you will thank me later.

Let's dive in!

THE BASICS: SMALL CHANGES MAKE HOCKEY STICKS

Hockey sticks? Yes—the kind in Figure 17.1:

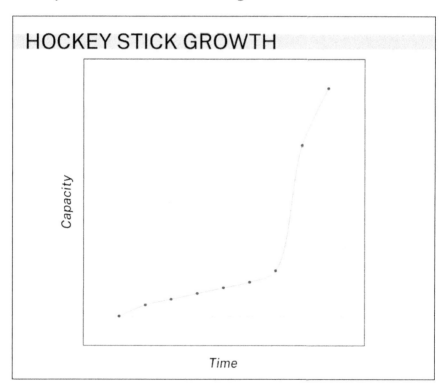

Figure 17.1: A growth chart is said to "hockey stick" when it makes a sharp turn up, signifying exponential growth.

When I was working in tech, "hockey stick growth" is what all the start-ups I worked with were after. It's where slow growth compounds, and then explodes, assuming you don't have bottlenecks that prevent it.

In the case of habits, the greatest potential bottleneck is mindset. Now you know why we spent so much time in the first three parts of this book. The other bottlenecks are a lack of tools or resources and making things too complex. You're about to learn how to solve for those and will have everything you need to quantum leap. And it'll start so small and manageable that you'll think there's a catch. (There's not!)

THE BEHAVIOR FORMULA: ACTS

In my experience, the most important concept in behavior design is knowing the four components that create every single habit. You can remember them by this aptly named acronym, ACTS. They are:

- Ambition (you want to do the behavior)
- Capability (whether or not you can do the behavior)
- Trigger (the prompt or cue to do the behavior)
- Satisfaction (the reward for doing the behavior)

Each is a precursor for what follows. You can be capable of doing a behavior, but you probably won't if you have no desire. Without a trigger to initiate the behavior, capability is moot. And there's no satisfaction unless the behavior is executed. See Figure 17.2.

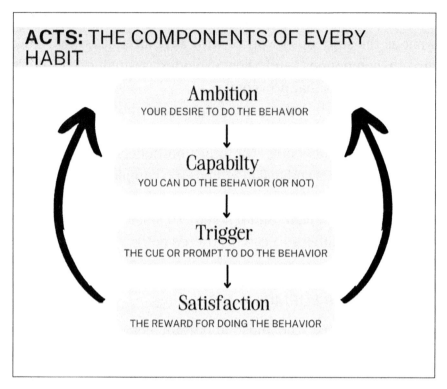

Figure 17.2: Each component in ACTS is a necessary precursor for what follows. It creates a positive feedback loop.

These components also create a feedback loop. Satisfaction increases our ambition, making us want to do the behavior again and again. (More on this soon.) This also has the downstream effect of increasing our capability as we repeat the behavior. So long as the trigger stays in place while we wire this behavior into automaticity, the behavior will become a habit.

As we explore each component in more detail, relate what you're reading to examples in your own life. This will lock in the learning and give you a head start when we start designing behaviors in the next chapter.

AMBITION

Ambition is the desire or motivation to do something. We typically give the most weight to ambition when creating habits, which is why we struggle with creating lasting ones. Because ambition and desire are feelings, they're transitory. They're relative, based on how much we feel like doing something from moment to moment.

Given that feelings change, this makes ambition a very poor foundation to build on. Perhaps you've felt motivated to get fit after the holidays, so you signed up for a gym membership. And maybe you stopped going shortly thereafter. If so, you've experienced motivation's unreliability firsthand. If you can relate to this example, you're not alone. Data from apps suggests a drop-off in exercise by the third week of January after a spike on the first days of the month.[73]

Taking the above example further, perhaps you stopped going to the gym because it was really cold outside, and you were more "motivated" to stay in a warm and cozy bed than you were to get up, get dressed, and scrape the ice off your windshield. Competing motivations like these happen every day. They compromise our success if we aren't aware of what's happening. You're about to learn how to redesign your behaviors to remove your feelings from the equation as much as possible. As discussed in earlier chapters, feeling our emotions is important. And yet, we must remember that we are the captain of our ship. If your emotions are currents that can take your ship off course, it's your role as captain to remain conscious and intentional. You must hold the wheel and maintain course to get where you want to go.

You'll sometimes experience conflicting desires, like wanting to stay in your warm and cozy bed while also wanting to go to the gym and work out. The following chapters will explain how to overcome these competing motivations through behavior design.

CAPABILITY

Capability is the most critical of the four components—not only for me but also for my clients. In general, if something is easy, we'll usually do it. But if there's friction or if it's difficult in *any* way, the odds of doing the behavior fall off a cliff. Let me give you a real-life personal example that may sound ridiculous but paints the picture of how even a tiny bit of friction makes a huge difference in whether or not you do a behavior.

Since I was a teenager, I've struggled with upper back pain. Specifically, knots under and around my shoulder blades. Long story short, it got bad enough that my left hand would go numb when I'd sleep on my left side, and the same on the right. Turns out, you can develop pseudo thoracic outlet syndrome from having muscles that are too tight. Sitting at a desk all day like I usually do is notorious for creating these issues.

Because "everything is always working out for me," I happened to marry a man with a graduate degree in kinesiology who worked as a physical therapist for many years. Jeff has helped me feel so much better by showing me specific stretches and foam rolling techniques. Alas, knowing the stretches and *doing them* are very different.

When you can't seem to do a desired behavior, ask yourself a question akin to magic: WTF ... *Where's the friction?* (I know you're not about to forget *that* acronym.)

When I asked myself where the friction was, I realized I wasn't foam rolling my shoulder blades because I have long hair, and it gets caught under the foam roller (and painfully pulled) unless I have my hair up. But I almost always have my hair down. The solution here was to put my hair up. Simple, right? But I wasn't doing it.

Here's where you peel back the layers of friction by asking the magic WTF question again. *Where's the friction with putting my hair up?*

Here is where the solution appeared. My hair clips and hair ties are kept in our bedroom. I foam roll in the family room, on the other side of the house. I have a beautiful home, but it's not exactly a sprawling estate like Versailles. It takes fifteen seconds to walk to my bedroom and get a hair tie or clip. But that was just enough friction to keep me from putting my hair up and foam rolling. A lasting solution? Keeping a hair tie or clip in a drawer close to where I foam roll. Simple! I'm willing to bet the capability factor and small bits of friction (with simple solutions) are all that's standing in your way of your desired habits too.

FACTORS THAT AFFECT CAPABILITY

Capability is critical in habit formation—both starting and stopping them. More on stopping them in Chapter 19, but keep this in mind as you read. Whether or not you're capable of taking a given action depends on factors across three buckets, which you can remember as (R *cubed*):

- Resources (time, money, tools, knowledge/skills, assistance)

- Rigor (how much work it is mentally, physically, and emotionally)
- Reach (whether it's within your reach to include the behavior into your existing day-to-day routine)

Recall the WTF question I asked myself when I wasn't foam rolling: *Where's the friction?* Let's look at the factors to find it.

In the foam rolling example, was it a missing *resource*?

Let's look at time first. It could be a time issue in certain situations, but in this case, no. I foam roll in the morning while the coffee brews and have at least five minutes, which is sufficient.

Was it tools? No, I already had the foam roller.

Was it money? No, I didn't need to buy anything.

Was it knowledge or skills? No, I knew how to foam roll because my husband taught me.

Was it assistance? No, I can do it on my own. (Of note, needing assistance to do a behavior is a red flag. If you want to make a behavior a habit, you'll have much better success if you can do it on your own.)

Now that we know it wasn't a resource problem, we move on to *rigor*.

Was it the amount of physical rigor? Yes! Though walking fifteen seconds into my bedroom doesn't sound like much work, it caused just enough friction to affect my capability.

Let's keep going for the sake of demonstrating this troubleshooting process.

How about mental rigor? If my husband hadn't shown me the stretches and techniques, this too, would've kept me from foam rolling. It takes mental effort to research, learn, and implement something new. Unless our ambition outweighs the required rigor, we won't do it. (More on this in a moment.)

Emotional rigor? No, and this won't always apply. (But here's an example to illustrate. Breathwork is a regular habit I'd like to create. I haven't done so because emotions always come up in breathwork, and I often don't have enough desire to outweigh the emotional rigor required.)

Finally, is foam rolling within *reach* of my current routine? Yes, our kitchen and family room are adjoined as a great room, so it's easy to foam roll while the coffee brews. If it fell outside of my current routine, I may have needed to make adjustments or find a better time and place to foam roll. (Maybe at the gym after a workout, for example.)

It can be harder to solve for gaps in resources like time and money. If rigor factors are to blame, you can strengthen these rather easily. This might mean making the physical action smaller or easier so it's less work.

For example, if you've never lifted weights and your desired behavior is bench pressing 200 pounds, that would be too physically rigorous. Perhaps you start with the bar or light dumbbells and work up from there as you get stronger.

If it's mental rigor, how can you make it less complex? Can you break it into smaller, simpler parts?

Sometimes, rigor factors can be solved with resources. Let's say you aren't bench pressing because you have a callous on your hand that opened and is physically painful. Weightlifting gloves could be a tool that makes you capable of doing the behavior. Or perhaps you don't lift weights because you're unsure which exercises and machines to use. Hiring a trainer or downloading an app to build your workouts could solve this problem. (I love the Fitbod app, another wonderful resource I can thank my husband for.)

Here's another personal example of a desired behavior I wasn't doing because I lacked capability factors. I only recently learned how to curl my hair. This was a problem because bad hair days kept me from feeling good about my appearance and often prevented me from filming content—a critical task for my business. In this example, I lacked resources in the form of knowledge, skills, and tools.

A solution I employed for a few months was getting a weekly blowout. That was great while it lasted, but then I lacked two other resources: time and money. I needed the time I spent driving and in the chair, and couldn't justify the cost. How could I do this at home to remove time and money from the equation?

The answer presented itself when a friend invited me to a hair curling class. I learned the proper technique (knowledge), and I got the correct tools—like a much better curling iron, a smoothing round brush, and the right styling products. It did take a small investment of time and money, as well as mental and physical rigor to attend the class and acquire the skills and tools, but it made me capable of doing this at home. Now it's a habit and part of my routine!

If you have a behavior you want to do but are struggling to perform, look at the factors. Which are you missing?

TRIGGER

The third component of every habit is the trigger, or what prompts or cues you to act. You can also think about triggers as opportunities to act or make a choice. Until your desired habit becomes an automatic behavior, the trigger is critical!

As an example, let's say you have a package being delivered that you are very excited to receive. It requires a signature. The delivery man comes to the door, but you're gardening in the backyard and don't hear the doorbell. He leaves, and you don't get your package that day.

In this case, you had the ambition to answer the door. You wanted the package! You had the capability. You were home and could've answered the door. But you missed the trigger.

Some examples of triggers are Post-it Note reminders in strategic places, vitamins on a pretty plate next to the coffee you drink without fail in the morning, a notification prompting you to open an app, or a reminder alarm on your phone.

We'll discuss this in more detail in Chapter 18, but one way to stop a habit is to remove the trigger. Let's say you want to stop your scroll. One way to avoid Instagram or TikTok altogether is to turn off the app notifications. No notifications mean no trigger, which gives you a leg up with lessening or stopping the behavior.

SATISFACTION

Satisfaction can take on different forms but always has the effect of making us want to repeat the behavior that caused it. This could be an internal reward—good feelings, a happy dance, an empowering visualization, or something else you do when things go your way. It can also be external, in the form of a reward.

Like satisfaction, external rewards can take many forms. The five love languages are a good example.[74] A reward could be verbal affirmation, an act of service, a material gift, a hug, or quality time. Another external reward is believing people perceive us in a positive way, whether we have evidence of that or not. The key is that the reward is directly tied to the behavior. More on this in a moment.

Celebration is critically important to habit formation because it wires in our new behaviors and does so faster. Celebration will begin to improve your entire life. It will shift your identity—and you know how critical that is to lasting change. You'll feel better about yourself and grow confident in the type of person you are becoming. Celebration helps create momentous feelings of success that snowball into *more* success. And I'm willing to bet it'll make you happier, too.

Through the lens of neuroscience, celebrating tiny changes and little wins does a couple of important things. First, you're using your reticular activating system (RAS) that we discussed in Chapter 5. As your brain's filter, when you place importance on celebrating, your RAS will go to work finding many things for you to celebrate—not just your new habits. Don't be surprised if you start celebrating short lines at Starbucks and green lights while driving. You'll probably attract more things to celebrate too.

The other reason celebration is so effective at wiring in a desired behavior is because it directly affects the reward center of our brains. *Celebration creates positive emotion, and positive emotion creates habits!*

The timing of celebration (or the reward) is critical for this to work, though. *You must celebrate the moment you remember to perform the behavior, while you do the behavior, or immediately (like, milliseconds) after doing it.* Timing is paramount because you must emotionally tie the celebration to the behavior. The more distance between the behavior and the reward, the less effective the reward will be at wiring in the behavior as a habit.

Let's say you're trying to stop swearing. If you go thirty days without uttering a curse word, you get to go on a shopping spree. This won't be nearly as effective as internally celebrating yourself for making a different choice of words whenever you remember to do so. Sure, you could do both, but in terms of turning a behavior into a habit, the immediate celebration is key. And it's free!

Consider the timing with external rewards as well. Let's use my daughter walking as an example. For some kids, a lot of positive reinforcement is needed to get them pumped up enough to walk. When Mila was a baby, I wore her in a carrier all the time. She loved it, and I think she would've continued that mode of transportation as long as I let her. When it came time for her to start walking, which finally happened at seventeen months, Jeff and I were like a hype crew every time she'd get into position. Even when she'd use a walker toy or stand on her own, we'd go crazy celebrating her. This totally helped her confidence (ambition, capability, and satisfaction in the behavior formula) and made her more interested in walking. And then when she took those first steps, we were like superfans sitting courtside at an NBA Finals game on the winning buzzer shot. She tied the reward of us celebrating to walking because it happened instantaneously. If we'd waited an hour or even five minutes, that tie-in wouldn't have happened. Forgive the comparison, but it's the same way with dog training. You *immediately* give a treat or a "good boy" and a pat on the head to reinforce a desired behavior, or the association between behavior and reward doesn't get made.

So how does this work? Celebrating causes your brain to release dopamine. We are all dopamine addicts ... or dopafiends. It's why we can't stop scrolling, eating cookies, or buying stuff online that we don't need. Dopamine doesn't discriminate between "bad" habits and "good" habits. If you deem a behavior pleasurable (even if it's "bad" for you), out flows that dopamine. When you celebrate a desired behavior, you hack this neural architecture to your benefit. Celebration encodes into your brain that doing your desired behavior makes you feel good— and you will want to get that feeling again and again, thus helping to form a habit.

Put another way to underscore this point, when we experience a surge of dopamine, our brain recognizes the sensation as pleasurable and rewarding. This triggers a learning process where the brain starts associating the activity that led to the dopamine release with positive feelings. Essentially, the brain is noting, *This activity made me feel good. Let's remember this for the future.* Over time, as this association strengthens, the behavior that triggered the dopamine release can become encoded as an automatic habit. (This is exactly why you may find yourself opening Instagram or another app unconsciously.)

Whether the satisfaction comes from inside or outside, it has the same effect in activating the brain's reward center. (If you're addicted to negative emotions like we discussed in Chapter 12, those emotions and their associated chemicals also serve as a reward.)

If you're like most people I've coached, you might bristle a little at celebrating upon performing a behavior that you think you "should" be doing anyway. But please, don't should on yourself, and don't skip this step!

Let me underscore the importance of this and the satisfaction component of the behavior formula. In my opinion, the best book that dives exclusively into behavior design is *Tiny Habits* by Dr. BJ Fogg. In fact, Dr. Fogg says, "If you learn just one thing from my entire book, I hope it's this: Celebrate your tiny successes."[75] *He literally wrote the book on behavior design and says celebration is the most important thing to learn!* You'll be a believer once you try it. Celebrate, celebrate, celebrate.

CAPABILITY IS KING (OR QUEEN)

Ambition and feelings of motivation can leave us high and dry when we need them most. It's why only 9 percent of people stick to their New Year's resolutions.[76] This is why we always prioritize capability in behavior design. Capability is reliable since it's compromised of the factors which are largely within our control. This makes capability an excellent foundation for building habits.

My preferred framework for behavior design is the ACTS model you read in this chapter. But there are other behavior change models and theories that may resonate with you more, or that are better suited for certain situations. They all have the same components; they're just ordered differently. I'll briefly explain each through a lens we can all relate to either through firsthand or secondhand experience: eating healthier. Note which of these approaches strike a chord with you, because this will help you design behaviors in the next chapter.

(And by the way, you can download the in-depth breakdown of these models and theories at alessiacitro.com/book.)

WHAT MOTIVATES AND SATISFIES YOU?

Are you the type of person whose ambition or desire to do a behavior increases as your capability does?[77] Us (recovering) perfectionists can relate to this. The better we are at something, the more likely we are to do it. If our *competence* is low, our motivation is low.

With healthy eating: This might mean you are not motivated to change your eating habits until you've learned all about macronutrients and which foods are best for you. It could also present as being unmotivated to cook until you've taken a class or learned some core recipes you love.

What about *autonomy*? Does doing something that's your idea satisfy you more than obligation, another's suggestion, or an external expectation? Think about something you have been asked or told to do. Can you *choose* whether or not you do it? If you can choose, are you *willing* to do it? If you have the ability to choose and you're willing, you will feel more satisfaction from the behavior.

With healthy eating: If it's your idea, eating well may feel very satisfying. If you're doing it because your partner hinted that you should, maybe not—unless you have agency to choose and are willing to do so. What if you're required to eat healthier by a doctor or for weight loss? When I was in my twenties, I worked with a bartender who commuted from Vegas to Chicago on the weekends. He told me that the bottle girls at some Vegas nightclubs were subjected to weigh-ins! If they gained weight, they'd be given a crappy section and get fired if they didn't lose the weight within a certain period. What a sexist and disgusting practice! If they needed the job, this would fall under the category of *not* having autonomy and being able to choose. And that is a sure way to kill satisfaction ... and crave Taco Bell instead of kale.

How about connection? If a behavior will make you feel more connected to others, does it increase your anticipated feelings of satisfaction?

With healthy eating: If all your friends eat super clean and you believe that doing so will improve your social life and make you more accepted, it will definitely increase your anticipated satisfaction. On the other side of the coin, if all your friends and family eat junk food, you may anticipate strained connections or being ridiculed, lowering your anticipated satisfaction and making you less likely to take up the behavior.

If you said yes to being more motivated when competent, autonomous, or connected to others, Self-Determination Theory may be the framework to apply when designing your new habits. This theory focuses on intrinsic motivations and the psychological needs of relatedness or connectedness, autonomy, and competence, which align nicely with the love and belonging, self-esteem, and self-actualization needs of Maslow's hierarchy.

There's one catch though for this model to work. Even if the anticipated satisfaction from a behavior is high, your capability (*competence*) must be adequate. If it is, your ambition (*motivation*) increases, and you will do the behavior. If it's not, you won't act and will spin your wheels. Another reason why capability is always the focus.

Self-Determination Theory starts with the trigger, or opportunity to do a behavior. Adequate anticipated satisfaction is likely present if you have the choice and willingness to do the behavior and if doing the behavior will lead to feelings of connectedness. You also need to feel capable of doing it. If these conditions are met, you will have sufficient ambition to do the behavior. This then becomes a feedback loop, with ambition to do the behavior (and doing it) creating higher levels of satisfaction and capability. You'll likely seek out more related triggers and opportunities too. (At the end of this chapter, I'll show you diagrams of all the theories and models side by side so you can easily see the differences between each.)

HOW MUCH DO REWARDS OR AVOIDING PUNISHMENT MOTIVATE YOU?

If you're really honest with yourself, how much is your behavior influenced by external outcomes? Specifically, outer rewards (money, likes on social, praise, recognition, gifts, etc.) or the avoidance of punishment and negative outcomes? We are *all* motivated by these factors, but which would you say is greater: your intrinsic motivation from feeling good, or from feeling agency and connection? Or the external motivation from satisfaction in gaining or avoiding something outside of you?

If external factors like this have a greater influence on you, Reinforcement Learning Theory may be the model to use in designing your habits. This theory says that we learn how to behave in a given situation by observing the outcomes (*punishment* or *reward*) of past behavior. Our brains crave satisfaction from rewards, reinforcing the behavior that led to the reward. We will adjust our behaviors to maximize rewards and minimize punishments.[78]

Here's what this model might look like with healthy eating:

- You're doing a detox with friends and there's money at stake. If you go the longest without a cheat meal, you'll win the cash and get bragging rights and recognition. You're externally motivated, and these rewards push you to keep eating clean.

- You hired a nutrition coach to hold you accountable. If you don't eat healthy every meal each week, your diet is made even stricter. This feels like punishment, and you follow the plan you've been given to the letter to avoid this.

I don't love this. It's like chasing a carrot on a stick. We're never fully satisfied and just keep chasing. And external motivators are rarely as meaningful and long-lasting as those that come from within. There are certainly "do-or-die" type scenarios where it can be a good fit. But I wouldn't leverage this model for long-term transformation. (I also bristle at this means of changing behavior because it reminds me of Pavlov's dogs, salivating at a bell ringing because they'd associated the sound with food. We are so much better than that!)

Reinforcement Learning Theory places emphasis on satisfaction from rewards, specifically learning from them and adjusting future behaviors to maximize rewards and avoid punishment. The more satisfaction you feel, the more ambition you have to do it, and so long as you remain capable and have continued opportunities, you'll do the behavior again and again.

The key weakness of Reinforcement Learning Theory and Self-Determination Theory is where they place emphasis: satisfaction, specifically rewards and punishment. The reward center of our brain and those feel-good chemicals are powerful, but putting satisfaction as the focal point in behavior design is a lot like putting yourself on a hamster wheel. In my experience personally and with clients, focusing on capability and trigger is a much more fulfilling and sustainable strategy.

WHERE ARE YOU NOW?

Which of the stages below aligns most closely to where you are *right now* in your journey to becoming your Higher Self?

1. You've almost finished this book, but change is not being considered, either due to denial or being unaware of your problems. Nothing is happening because ambition and capability aren't there. You're still unaware of the triggers presenting themselves as well as the satisfaction you could experience from change.

2. You're aware of changes you could make, and you're thinking about starting within the next six months. While aware of the pros and cons of your status quo, you have insufficient capability or ambition to act. This is why you haven't started yet and are "thinking" about it.

3. You plan to make a change within the next month. You've likely made the decision to move forward and may have gotten started with small steps. Your ambition has increased, and now the focus moves to increasing capability. You're anticipating satisfaction but maybe haven't experienced it yet.

4. You're in action! This is where specific and observable behavior changes take place, thanks to the presence of all four components of ACTS. Way to go!

5. You've ascended into a higher version of yourself. You're focused on preventing relapse and consolidating the gains you've made. This stage is about continuing your new behaviors until they become habits, while avoiding returning to old behaviors. Maintaining satisfaction is key here as the habit is wired in, so you're dialed in on celebrating your wins. The trigger for your behavior may become less important in this stage.

6. You've arrived at one of two end points. If the temptation to revert to your old behaviors is no longer felt, your new behavior has become a firmly rooted habit. Congratulations! Alternatively, the old behavior may have happened again. This can reduce capability and affect ambition. Satisfaction with your new and improved way of life might diminish. This would prompt a return to an earlier stage.

If you've made it this far in the book, there is no way you're at Stage 1. Stages 3–4 are most likely, but wherever you are is right for you. Has reading this book helped you advance a stage or two? If so, give yourself major kudos!

The model you just went through is the Transtheoretical Model (TTM) of Behavior Change.[79] I love this model as a means of zooming out and viewing the whole process, and because it uses ACTS. Things don't get rolling until all four of the ACTS components are present. There's a lot of value to viewing behavior change this way, because yes, we can begin designing behaviors with all these components, but it took you progressing through the first three stages (whether you realized it or not) to have all four available to you.

Here's what each stage might look like with healthy eating:

1. Precontemplation: You're unaware or in denial that you could feel or look better than you do right now. All you know are processed, unhealthy foods. You may think, *this is just the way it is.*

2. Contemplation: You're aware of how you could go about eating better and how it would benefit you, but you're not sure you have the capability (the R-cubed factors) or the motivation to see it through and get started.

3. Preparation: You're more motivated and have made the decision to start, but not yet. You're working on increasing your capability through things like finding healthy recipes, getting kitchen equipment, and watching videos to teach you cooking basics. You may be experiencing satisfaction through increased self-confidence and energy, but not necessarily. (Unless, of course, you have a habits coach who taught you to celebrate the tiny progress and wins!)

4. Action: You're forging ahead, putting it all together. You're seeing results and experiencing the good feelings that come with progress!

5. Maintenance: You've reached a level you feel wonderful about, and now your focus shifts to maintaining your gains and locking in your lifestyle change for permanent results. You may also feel motivated to take on another challenge and area of growth.

6. Termination or Relapse: Your new lifestyle has indeed become a way of life! You look and feel better than you ever have before. Or alternatively, you had a "cheat meal" that completely derailed you. It caused you to fall out of the habit of healthy eating. When you have adequate ambition to resume this habit, you'll pick back up at an earlier stage.

Let's view the above examples of the six TTM stages through the lens of ACTS. None are present in the Precontemplation stage. ACTS are present in Contemplation, but none to sufficient levels. And remember, capability is what causes action! Preparation has all four, but there is not enough of any one to initiate consistent behavior. Action is where the habits magic starts to happen, with enough of each component. Maintenance is where the habit becomes wired in, so long as the past behavior isn't resumed. The final stage can take one of two paths: termination or relapse. Termination means the new habit is firmly rooted and will happen with little to no effort. Relapse means the old behavior was resumed and the individual needs to pick back up at a previous stage, depending on the level of relapse.

YOUR HIGHER SELF "ACTS" THE PART

Now that you know a few different ways to go about behavior change, let's explore some facets of ACTS that are illuminated by The Fogg Behavior Model.[80] If you want more after reading this book, I highly recommend grabbing a copy of *Tiny Habits* where Dr. BJ Fogg explores this in great depth.

In the Fogg Model, satisfaction is the C in his ABC acronym for when and how to do a new behavior. You attach your new behavior to an existing automatic habit (an Anchor), you perform the Behavior, and you Celebrate. If you've read *Atomic Habits* by James Clear, you may be familiar with anchoring as "habit stacking."[81]

In his model, Dr. Fogg makes a very powerful simplification in the relationship between ambition and capability. He asserts that they are compensatory, meaning that if one is high, the other can be low, and we may still be able to do the behavior.

A story of teenage sisters in Oregon provides a great example.[82] In 2013, Jeff Smith got trapped under his 3,000-pound tractor, the weight of which was on his chest. Somehow, he wasn't crushed and was able to scream for help. His thirteen- and sixteen-year-old daughters, Haylee and Hannah, heard his screams and ran to try and save him. The two young girls were able to lift the tractor, saving their father's life.

How capable are normal teenage girls of lifting a 3,000-pound tractor? Probably not very. But how much ambition did they have to lift it and save their dad? A ton—a ton and a half to be exact. In this example, the *ambition* (and flood of adrenaline) was great enough to compensate for a lack of capability, enabling the Smith sisters to lift the tractor off their dad.

But imagine the sisters want to start lifting tractors as part of their fitness routine. Their ambition won't be high enough to compensate for the difficulty. It is too physically rigorous for them to be capable of doing this as a regular feat. This would make it unlikely for tractor-lifting workouts to become a reliable, repeated behavior. We'll dive into this concept more in Chapter 18 when you begin designing your own behaviors.

The inverse of the relationship between ambition and capability is also true. You can have little to no ambition or desire to do a behavior, but if it's easy enough, you'll remain capable and might still do it.

Here's how ACTS and The Fogg Model might look with healthy eating:

- You have the ambition and desire to eat nutritious food.
- You shore up your capability to do so by gathering the necessary resources (like cooking and kitchen prep tools, recipes, meal plans, etc.) and figuring out how to weave them into your routine.
- You create a prompt or cue to meal prep and grocery shop when you say you want to, such as a reminder on your phone and a Google Calendar reminder.

- You celebrate every time you eat healthy and, as a result, feel deeply satisfied!

WHICH MODEL OR THEORY IS BEST FOR YOU?

Cater to your *intrinsic* desire. Most of you reading this, myself included, have been on a hamster wheel of external motivations for way too long. In general, doing something driven by external expectations and demands isn't fun, fulfilling, or energizing. You're reading this book because you are internally motivated! Lean into that!

Avoid motivating yourself through external outcomes (Reinforcement Learning Theory) unless it's do-or-die, and avoiding punishment or negative outcomes is the only way you can rally yourself to act. If you take this route, I urge you to really lean into the satisfaction component, celebrating the shit out of every win, no matter how tiny.

Be cautious if autonomy and capability are your intrinsic motivators (Self-Determination Theory). This way of behavior change has conditions and plays into perfectionist tendencies. Remember, in this model, you feel ambition *if* you are capable. Sounds a lot like waiting until you feel ready, if you ask me.

I like TTM in that it breaks down the stages of lasting change and uses the same formula of ACTS. What I *don't* like about it is the emphasis on avoiding "bad" behavior. But, if your domino habit is like mine (drinking too much), it might be a great model to help you break it down into smaller pieces and create a new habit while staying focused on avoiding the one you're trying to kick.

I'm partial to ACTS and The Fogg Model, but whichever theory or model you choose, know you have the permission to pivot and try a different model at any point in this process. If you feel successful right away, it's a sign you picked a great starting point.

Figures 17.3 through 17.6 show the models and theories next to each other so you can see the variances.

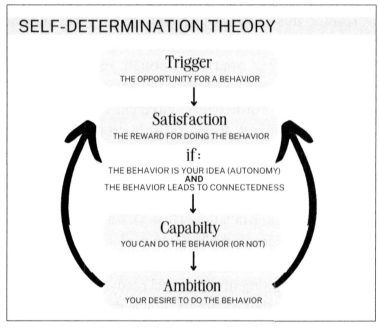

Figure 17.3: Self-Determination Theory.

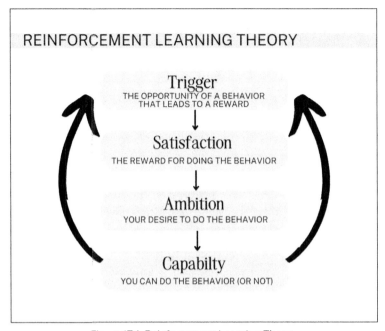

Figure 17.4: Reinforcement Learning Theory.

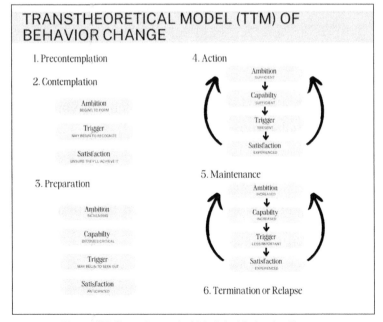

Figure 17.5: Transtheoretical Model of Behavior Change.

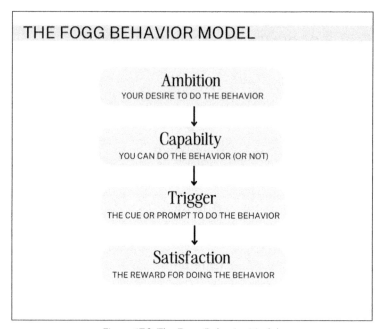

Figure 17.6: The Fogg Behavior Model.

BE HER NOW EXERCISE:

Write down which models resonated with you the most (and for which behaviors). Which are you being intuitively called to try first?

And with that, we are moving on to designing your new habits!

Chapter 18

Crafting Habits to Create Your Dream Life

"Rituals are the formulas by which harmony is restored."

— Terry Tempest Williams

Action is where the rubber meets the road in bringing forth our desired realities. Keeping in mind the energy of our Higher Selves and how we are *being*, let's dive into how to design the behaviors that will 3D print this version of you into existence. But first ...

HABITS AREN'T BORING—AND YOU WON'T BE EITHER

Many of us—including me, for years—avoid creating positive habits because we think our lives will become boring and devoid of fun. If you're a woman reading this book, I'm willing to bet you're high achieving, type A (+), and you're very comfortable in your "doing" energy, to the point that adding more structure sounds fucking miserable. *I've been there, and I understand.*

Or maybe you love spontaneity, and you're worried habits will constrain you.

Here's the truth: habits set you free to do more of what you love and what lights you up like a firework on the Fourth of July.

Yes, habits provide structure. But think of habits as a glass and the things you love to do as water. They need each other. Without the glass, the water goes all over the table. Rather than quenching your thirst like it was meant to, the spilled water makes a mess. It fries your laptop that was on the table. Its mess creates chaos. As a glass does for water, the supportive structure of positive habits creates the freedom for you to go with the flow, flourish, create, and do what you were meant—and love—to do. Coming full circle to the opening chapter, this is having masculine and feminine energies in balance. This is where we thrive—and how habits don't feel like a drag.

The Western world has us "programmed to see life as drab and colorless, an endless trek through a meaningless series of obstacles"[83] if we adopt routines. That's exactly how I used to feel about mundane and repetitive habits, but they don't need to be boring, strict, and rigid.

The above quote continues: "As your Life Force gets stronger, you begin to see beauty everywhere—a living breathing spirit and an ever-present source of inspiration." This is *exactly* how habits have opened my world. I'm willing to bet it'll be the same for you.

We can either be in a state of expansion or contraction—never both at once. If the habits you adopt feel constrictive or suffocating, keep tweaking them until they make you feel expansive and free. Once you learn and begin playing with behavior design, you'll see how easy it is to make adjustments that work for *you.*

CLARIFY YOUR ASPIRATIONS AND OUTCOMES

Take the needs you want to solidify from the audit stage and get specific on your goals. For precision, "goals" can be the outcomes you desire versus more general aspirations you have. They're similar but have a key distinction: specificity. With your initial goals, I recommend focusing on outcomes rather than aspirations. Here's why. Aspirations are abstract and broad, like wanting to be successful in your career. Outcomes, meanwhile, often take the form of SMART goals, meaning they're specific, measurable, achievable, relevant, and time bound. Put another way, outcomes happen by repeatedly executing the correct behaviors, while aspirations are realized by outcomes stacked over time.

An aspiration might be wanting to be an author someday. An outcome is becoming a published author by a certain date. Including aspirations in this process is fine, as they're high-level and visionary. However, I like focusing on specific outcomes first because the target is clear and can easily be broken down into smaller pieces.

For simplicity's sake, I'll use "goal" from here on out, but keep the difference between outcomes and aspirations in mind. This will inform how detailed and precise you need to be, and whether we're talking big picture or more immediate focus.

Most importantly, choose goals that are meaningful to you. Focus on ones that affirm your desired identity. Regardless of what you start with, meaningful and impactful goals help you avoid conflicting motivations and the psychological pain of cognitive dissonance. This will make becoming your Higher Self easier—in the short term and long term.

To clarify what you're aiming for, if you aspire to become your Higher Self, what does that mean, specifically? What does it look like? Is it a feeling or a state of being? Is it a set of life circumstances? Is it a specific outcome—or several? Once you've created clarity, you can start designing the behaviors to take you there. Imagine your goal as a destination and behavior design as the GPS.

BE HER NOW EXERCISE:

Answer the questions in the above paragraph with specificity. What are the goals you most want to achieve?

DESIGNING YOUR FIRST BEHAVIOR

If you aren't sure which goal to start with, choose one that doesn't cause pain or carry emotional baggage (like losing weight might, for example). And choose something you're excited about that's relatively easy. Focusing on capability (how easily you can do something) is a great focus point because in most cases, it remains the same or improves. Starting with something that you're also excited about is an effective way to get the ball rolling, but remember, we don't want to rely on ambition and motivation when designing behavior because they can be fickle; their presence is welcome, but consider it a bonus.

Once you have your clear goal, we'll reverse-engineer into the behaviors to achieve it. Consider your clear goal now while you see how the design process works in practice. To illustrate, we'll use an aspiration many of us share: to cook at home more often.

Step 1: Brainstorm behaviors.

List as many behaviors as you can think of that could help you achieve your goal. At this stage, nothing is too optimistic or unrealistic.

Some examples you come up with might include buying a set of kitchen knives, getting new cookbooks, hiring a personal chef, meal planning and prepping twice a week, etc. Some behaviors will be one-time (like buying cookbooks or knives). Others will be new habits you'll need to create or existing ones to continue or expand on. You may also list behaviors you could stop, like canceling your DoorDash subscription to discourage you from ordering takeout.

The more ideas, the better. Recruit other people to help you brainstorm. Ask your partner, colleagues, or your kids for help. You can even post to social media and ask for suggestions. Your list can include far-out and ridiculous ideas. The point is to get as many down as you can—ideally ten to twenty-five.

Before moving on to the next step, go through your list and make the behaviors more specific. For instance, if meal planning is on your list, think through how you'd do it and make it more specific by saying something like "meal plan twice a week: on Saturday morning and Tuesday evening."

I've said this before, but it bears repeating: Difficulty in sticking to a habit is not a *you* problem. It's a behavior design problem. This is why this next step is so important.

Step 2: What will move the needle? And what do you want to do?

Take your list and select the best behaviors *for you.* Remember two of the components in the ACTS behavior formula: ambition and capability. You must be capable of doing the behavior. Critically, you must also be able to get yourself to do it. Circle the behaviors you want to do, that feel easy-ish, and that you can do.

The final consideration is effectiveness. Is the behavior actually going to help? Or will it just add one more thing to your already long to-do list? Go through your list and put a line through any behaviors that probably won't move the needle. You can always come back and reassess if needed.

If you're going back and forth on whether you're motivated to consistently do the behavior in question, ask yourself: Do I *actually want to do this?* We already know that "should-ing" on ourselves doesn't work. Willpower and motivation are fair-weather friends, at best. And when they desert us, we don't do the behavior, and then we feel shame. Do you remember the emotional frequency scale from Chapter 11? Shame is as low vibe as it gets, besides being dead. That's not how we transform and become our Higher Selves. We are going for *feeling good!* Get laser-focused and unapologetic on what you already desire to do, versus what you think you *should* do.

Look back at your list. Your circled behaviors without a line through them are the ones to consider putting into practice. As always, approach these with curiosity, as if you're experimenting—because you are! You'll likely revise or abandon some behaviors as you see what works and what doesn't. That's to be expected and part of the process. Remember to have fun with this and pivot as needed.

By selecting behaviors that are effective, that you want to do and can do, you are setting yourself up for success. Like we've discussed before, success begets success and snowballs as your confidence grows.

If you're a recovering perfectionist or highly competitive, you might initially scoff at this because you feel the need to "challenge" yourself. But—and I say this with love—you're reading this book because something's not working, right? I initially felt the same way and resisted this part of the behavior design process. I thought this seemed too easy. That if something wasn't hard or didn't require willpower, it was probably too insignificant to matter, anyway. But that's just Pam, at it again. If I'm reading your mind right now, I'd like to lovingly remind you that life can be full of ease and flow ... *if we believe it can be*. Let this be an experiment in ease.

IMPLEMENTATION

You have your starting behaviors—now what? Review each. Are any of them one-time tasks? In the cooking at home example, perhaps it's a kitchen tool purchase or a skill acquisition, like taking a cooking class. If it feels aligned and you can do it now, do those one-time behaviors first to create momentum and strengthen as many R-cubed factors as possible. (For review: Resources, Rigor, and Reach.)

Next, which repeated behaviors will you need to implement? Choose one or two to begin with. Now comes a very important question: How can you scale these repetitive behaviors back?

When I first became a student of habits, I read somewhere that to start a habit of walking or working out, you should begin by creating the habit of putting your shoes on. That's it. Nothing more. I thought this was ridiculous! But success leaves clues, and it's effective. If you put your shoes on, you'll probably do more, like walk to the mailbox or down the block. But even if you don't do more—if you just put on your shoes—you create a baseline habit you can maintain come hell or high water. This wires it in. And importantly, you remove perfectionist pressure and make yourself more likely to succeed. When putting your shoes on feels like a breeze, then you can scale up a bit. (Scaling up might look like walking to the mailbox, then down the block. The key is to keep the baseline low so you can do it no matter what.)

By starting itty bitty like this, you accomplish two things. Yes, you create a baseline you can maintain regardless of what's happening in your life. But perhaps more importantly, you create feelings of success. Keeping promises to ourselves is how we build confidence. Keep the promises small so they can grow and blossom, and watch your confidence reach new heights. This is how you create the energy to ultimately tackle bigger and bigger behaviors that pave the way for quantum leaps.

CUE IT UP

Once you've scaled back your behavior and made it itty bitty, look at your day and your existing routines. What are the things you do daily without conscious thought? These are the perfect places on which to layer your new habits.

With my coaching clients, I've seen time and again that this exercise is more difficult than it sounds. The reliable, deeply rooted habits that happen on autopilot often get done without conscious thought, making them harder to recall than you'd think. To solve for this, go through a typical day in your mind. From the moment you wake up until bedtime, write down every single daily action. List them in the order you do them. If you have a hard time thinking of them all, that's okay. If you think of more later, you can add and adjust as needed.

Now, where does it make sense to do your new behavior? Consider existing routines that the new behavior would fit into seamlessly. Account for the spaces and places these routines happen in too. If adding your new behavior is even remotely inconvenient—like the hair tie down the hall that kept me from foam rolling—it's unlikely you'll make this behavior a habit. Think of it this way: you must plant these habit seeds in ideal conditions to grow. If you wouldn't plant a garden in your basement, don't plant your habit seeds out of reach of your current routines.

The other reason for pairing new behaviors with existing habits is that the existing routine can help to serve as a trigger. But we're going to take it a step further with an actual cue or prompt. "Out of sight, out of mind" is a phrase we've all heard and know for a reason. Because it's true. When you're looking to begin a new habit, the trigger to do it is imperative!

Triggers can take many forms. They can be a phone reminder alarm, a calendar alert, a Post-it Note, a fridge stocked with fruits and veggies, running shoes by the bed, or a front-and-center place on your desk for urgent items. You get the idea. Play with different cues and see what works best for you.

Likewise, if you're looking to stop a behavior, remove the trigger. For example, if you don't want to get sidetracked while working, close all your open browser tabs or get a tool that will hide them. If you don't want to eat junk food, remove it from your home, or put it in the back of the pantry so you don't see it when you're hungry and looking for a snack. Again, "Out of sight, out of mind." Use it to your advantage.

MAKE IT EASIER (OR HARDER) TO DO

As you experiment with implementing your new habits, continually look for ways you can make them easier to do.

Here's a personal example. I wanted to create the habit of making a protein smoothie every day. When we lived in an apartment, I was struggling to regularly do this. There were several ingredients, and adding all the different powders to the smoothie was time-consuming and messy. When I was done adding collagen, creatine, fiber, cacao, and protein, my counter looked like Scarface had been there. Our storage situation sucked and, it took time to take all the containers out and to put them all back. The R-cubed factors inhibiting my capability were physical rigor and time. How could I solve for them?

Armed with the knowledge of behavior design, we moved into our home, and I made it as easy as possible. I dedicated an entire drawer to protein smoothies, with everything organized inside. I got glass containers large enough to hold all the powder ingredients so I could portion them out ahead of time. Adding all the powders for one smoothie into a single container and preparing all my ingredients for the week at once saved me a ton of time and cut down on the mess each time I made a smoothie. When I'd go to make one, I only needed one scoop of powder, frozen fruit, and almond milk—it was easy to do.

Years before this, I also struggled to make smoothies regularly, but for a different reason. Then, it was because I absolutely hated handwashing our blender. Here we ask ... WTF? (Where's the friction?) Washing a blender is simple, but it created enough friction thanks to slightly too much physical rigor and the time it took to do it. I began working with a nutritional coach who introduced me to the Nutribullet. To this day, it's one of my favorite kitchen appliances, ever. With the Nutribullet, I can blend my smoothie in the same cup I drink it from. I just need to put the cup in the dishwasher when I'm done and can quickly rinse off the blade. Easy!

Now, the obstacles I mentioned that made it hard for me to make smoothies don't sound like a big deal, do they? This is why it's easy to shame ourselves about not doing a given behavior. We say things to ourselves like, *How hard is it to wash a blender? Why can't I just do it?* But here's the thing—we are all spinning so many plates that it takes very little friction, difficulty, or inconvenience to make us *not* do something. This doesn't mean we're weak, lazy, or suck at life. It means we're human, doing the best we can with what we've got and the neural architecture we were endowed with. Focus on making things as easy as possible and watch how good you'll feel—and how much more you'll *want* to do. This is how we acquire what we desire.

Likewise, if you want to *stop* doing a behavior, make it harder to do.

Case in point: I have yet to meet someone who doesn't want to spend less time on their phone, especially in bed or in the morning upon waking. The best solution to stop this behavior is to make it harder to use your phone. I use two solutions to accomplish this, both of which work effectively.

The first is to get a ridiculously short charging cord. I'm not kidding, the one I plug into on my nightstand is six inches long. This hits all four components of the ACTS behavior formula: ambition, capability, trigger, and satisfaction. You likely have more desire to wake up to a fully charged phone than you do to unplug it and scroll, especially if you have to fuss with finding and plugging back into a short little cord in the dark. And, unless you have really long arms, you probably can't scroll on a phone that's charging on a six-inch cable, so your capability is gone. The six-inch cable also removes the trigger because it's plugged into a port inside my drawer. I can't *see* my phone when it's charging. Out of sight, out of mind. This checks the satisfaction box too. You'll sleep better from not staring at blue light and feel good because you did what you said you wanted to.

The second solution to stop the morning scroll is the one I like even more. I do this one when my husband is home and not traveling for work, which is when I feel comfortable having my phone outside of the bedroom. When he's home, I charge my phone in my office at night. This again hits all four behavior components. I'm far more motivated to stay in my warm and cozy bed than I am to get up, walk into another room, and get my phone. The phone being in another room also greatly lowers my capability to use it. This also removes the trigger. And again, it's extremely satisfying to sleep well and do what you say you want to do. I like this solution best because it also lowers my likelihood of getting on my phone after I get out of bed in the morning.

I have a bonus solution for this common phone problem. Any time we can interrupt an undesired behavior with conscious thought, it's easier to stop ourselves from doing it. That might look like employing a trigger that forces thought or presence. Like putting a Post-it on your screen with a loving reminder that you don't want to use your phone for at least thirty minutes after waking. Without the note, you likely would've gotten on your phone unconsciously. With the note, you'll stop and think, giving you the ability to make a conscious choice. Or if it's stopping your scroll at night, maybe you log out of Instagram. To log back in, you'd need to manually key in a highly complex password that you have no shot at memorizing. Bringing conscious awareness and increasing mental rigor are great ways to stop yourself from doing undesired behaviors.

MAKE HABITS TAKE ROOT FASTER

If you want to wire in your new habits faster, here are a few very effective ways to do so.

Mental Rehearsal

Mentally rehearse or imagine doing the behavior seven to ten times. Include the celebration too! As discussed in Chapter 10, our brains do not know the difference between vividly imagined experiences and those that have actually happened. Use this to your advantage.

You can also use this to help you stop a behavior. When I quit drinking, this worked powerfully. If I was going to a social gathering, I'd imagine myself walking into the party and would mentally rehearse declining a cocktail and opting for a nonalcoholic beverage instead. Whatever you typically fall prey to or cave in on, try mental rehearsal to strengthen your muscle of saying no. I think you'll be surprised how well you'll handle the temptation the next time it pops up in real life.

Use Scent and Sound

Leveraging scent is a potent way to manipulate your neural architecture to your advantage. Your olfactory system is what governs your ability to smell. It's directly linked to your limbic system. (Remember when we talked about layers of the brain in Chapter 5? This is the mid-layer of the brain, which governs emotion.) Within your brain, your olfactory bulb is next door to the amygdala and hippocampus.

The amygdala is chiefly responsible for processing and storing emotions. When you smell a scent you've encountered before and have an emotional association with it, your amygdala evaluates the scent's emotional significance and activates the emotional response linked to its stored memory. Depending on the triggered memory, you might respond to the scent stimulus with negative emotions like anxiety or fear or positive emotions like happiness or joy.

The hippocampus forms and retrieves memories. It helps you recall the specific details and context of the memory associated with a scent. This is why a specific smell can take you to a particular memory or moment in time.

One of my favorite scents is the smell of fresh-cut grass. It takes me right back to my grandparents' Iowa farm, and I feel happy, free, playful, and joyful. In this example, my hippocampus retrieved the details: the people and place. My amygdala surfaced the associated feelings.

To use scent in habit formation, reflect on the people, places, and activities that make you feel most optimal. If you want to feel relaxed and you always feel peak relaxation at a particular vacation spot, can you buy the hand soap that your favorite resort stocks and use it at home? This is a real example—I order Mālie Organics Koke'e hand soap for our bathroom, and every time I wash my hands, it takes me right back to the Andaz Maui. I immediately feel the rush of those happy neurochemicals.

If you miss your partner while they're traveling, can you spray their fragrance on the pillow? If you miss your grandma, can you bake the cookies she always made and fill your home with their smell? If you want to summon feelings of empowerment, possibility, and capability, do you have a special scent you wear to important meetings or conferences that can bring you back into that emotional state?

Music functions much the same way in eliciting emotions and memories, with a few differences. For one, music is processed by the auditory complex and tends to evoke more explicit and autobiographical memories. The memories tied to a particular song might be more detailed and narrative, tied to specific events or periods in life. The range of emotions may be broader too, partly because music is more complex than scent.

Also noteworthy is how music is deeply intertwined with social and cultural contexts. This is why a walk-up song might summon more feelings of power and courage before speaking to an audience than a specific scent might. The music engages you *and* the audience by leveraging the song's cultural context and shifting the atmosphere within the environment.

Now, let's put it all together. What are scents you can tap into to achieve your desired emotional states? What music aligns with these feelings? Diffuse those scents or light a candle. Play the music before or while performing the behavior you want to wire in. Using scent and sound creates a multisensory association; over time, the music or the scent can serve as a cue to do the behavior. Music and scent can do double duty too, effectively serving as their own reward by triggering dopamine and the emotional state that gets you into aligned action.

I regularly use scent and sound and leaned into both for writing this book. I paired a specific perfume and room spray with the same exact songs every time I got ready to sit down and write. It got me into a feeling of possibility and empowerment. And while I'd write, I'd play binaural beats or Gregorian chants for focus. This signaled to my brain that it was time to write and evoked the emotional state necessary for inspired writing. These practices would make the emotions of *being* my Higher Self wash over me. I'd *be her now* and get excited to write! If you haven't tried this, consider this your invitation to choose your Higher Self signature scent and walk-up song. (Speaking of, you might like the playlist I created for this book. Check it out at alessiacitro.com/book.)

GROWTH AND REVISITING DOMINO HABITS

When you're crushing it and wiring in your new habits, a natural question to ask is when it's the right time to expand a habit from its itty-bitty baseline version. The answer is it depends. Consider these two criteria to decide. One, make a habit bigger when its itty-bitty version has become automatic. Two, and more importantly, expand the habit when you *want* to.

Note some habits will have a cap on their growth. Let's say cleaning your whole kitchen once a week is a habit you want to adopt, and you start with one counter. Eventually, you will have scaled up to clean the whole thing—and then you've maxed out. Unless you remodel and expand your kitchen, you've reached the cap on that habit.

Then there are habits that multiply, another way you can leverage the concept of *domino habits*. We discussed these in Chapter 16, but here's a quick refresher. A domino habit is one that naturally expands and creates other habits. For example, if you create a habit of going to the gym, you're probably also creating habits like drinking more water, eating better, and cooking at home more often. Here, the gym is the domino habit.

If you want to create a domino habit, choose one that *adds* to your life like the gym in the example above. Don't start this process with *stopping* a domino habit. And yes, I know I started my journey with stopping a domino habit—drinking alcohol—but it's easier to *add* a habit than to *subtract* it. More on stopping habits in the next chapter, but for now, focus on *starting* habits to build your confidence and momentum.

BE HER NOW EXERCISE:

Armed with everything you need to design behaviors, what are you committing to putting into action immediately? What are you excited to start with? How are you going to make it itty bitty?

Chapter 19

Bless and Release Negative Habits

"Refusing to release often means refusing to have peace. When we release in peace, we signal we're now ready to receive what's meant for this season, right now."

—Lysa TerKeurst

On the road to becoming our Higher Selves, there are going to be behaviors we need to say goodbye to. The good news is, there's help.

THE UNIVERSE HAS YOUR BACK IN LETTING "BAD" HABITS GO

Leverage a metaphysical law of the universe, the law of vacuum. Nature abhors a vacuum, meaning empty or void spaces are naturally filled. In a metaphysical sense, this concept can be applied to various aspects of our lives, whether it's habits, relationships, material possessions, jobs, or personal environments.

Dr. Jenn Chrisman introduced this to me as I struggled to let my wine business go. She shared a key component of this law with me: that the energy in which we let something go is the energy in which the void will be filled.

Keeping this in mind, let your "bad" habits go without judging them or yourself. Let them go in love and gratitude for the lessons they provided and for the insight into *who you are not*.

From the perspective of how this law works, consider the following before ditching any habits:

Create Space for the New: The law of vacuum suggests that to bring in new, positive experiences or habits, there must be space for them. This means letting go of old, negative, or unproductive habits to create room for better ones.

Intentional Replacement: When you consciously let go of a bad habit, it's important to replace it—intentionally—with a positive one. If you don't fill that vacant space with a chosen habit, it might get filled with another detrimental behavior.

Mindful Awareness: Be mindful of what you are creating space for. Letting go of a habit isn't only about removal; it's about preparing for what you wish to attract or manifest in its place.

Embrace Change: This is an opportunity to embrace change and growth. It's a reminder that letting go is not simply an end but a necessary step toward new beginnings. (And isn't that why you're reading this book?)

IT'S NOT ABOUT BREAKING, IT'S ABOUT UNWINDING

I invite you to throw the phrase "breaking a bad habit" into the trash bin of your mind. To stop doing something that is deeply ingrained, it's a gradual unwinding—not a one-and-done event as the term "breaking" implies.

Before we go further, it's important to note the methods in this chapter are not suitable as a treatment for serious addictions. Addiction is a complex condition that often requires professional intervention, including medical treatment, counseling, and support from qualified healthcare professionals. If you or someone you know is struggling with addiction, it is crucial to seek professional help. The information in this book should not be used as a substitute for professional advice, diagnosis, or addiction treatment. You can find resources in the Appendix to point you in the right direction.

That said, if you have bad habits that are *not* serious addictions, the unwinding method below is for you.

Do you remember when you were in elementary school and kids would twist the swings around and around, getting the chains all wound up? Think back to what you had to do if you wanted to go on the swing after this took place. You had to unwind it, rotation by rotation, until the chain became completely unkinked and unwound. Or what about when you've wrapped the cord around your hair dryer a few too many times, and the cord gets tight and twisted? How do you loosen it? You hold onto the top of the cord with the hair dryer hanging down, letting it spin and unwind itself. In either of these examples, would pulling harder work? No. Would cutting the chain or the hair dryer cord work? No. This is exactly why "breaking" a habit doesn't work and why it's a misnomer. To stop a habit, you approach it the same way as the swing or the hair dryer cord: you unwind it, and let gravity help you. In this case, gravity is akin to momentum and the easiest "bad" habits that contribute to the larger one you're solving for.

PHASE 1: CREATE THE VOID

What new habit are you creating to replace the one you want to stop? If you haven't started any of your new desired behaviors yet, keep reading but pause for now on unwinding any unwanted habits. Seeing success in creating new habits first will make unwinding bad habits easier. Trust me on this.

The other reason for focusing first on habits that create a gain is that, as we've covered thoroughly, your identity governs everything. Making positive changes will begin to change your identity, and your thermostat setting will rise. This alone will automatically begin to eliminate some of your unwanted habits. If you begin to step into the identity of your Higher Self, you'll want to stop doing many behaviors that are misaligned without much fuss or effort.

Lastly, why does it matter to you to unwind this particular habit? Yes, motivation is fickle, but having your *why* at the ready will bring increased clarity—and can only help you.

PHASE 2: USE BEHAVIOR DESIGN TO STOP A HABIT

Here we leverage all components of the ACTS behavior formula: ambition, capability, trigger, and satisfaction. You can play with adjusting these and see which helps you unwind most effectively. You can reduce your desire to do the behavior, lessen your capability to do it, remove the trigger, or make it less satisfying. The good news is that you may only need to affect one component to stop the undesired habit.

Use the following process to stop habits like watching TV, snacking too much, or scrolling social media for hours on end.

Consider the overall habit you want to stop. Make a list of every behavior that contributes to doing it. Start by writing, "I want to stop _____ [the overall habit]." Let's use the example of snacking too much on unhealthy foods.

Now, which specific behaviors contribute to the overall habit you want to stop? Continuing with the above snacking example, here might be some contributing behaviors:

- You lack time to prepare a healthy snack.
- You or your partner stock the pantry with unhealthy snacks.
- You're on the road a lot. You grab a snack while you're on the go, and there aren't many healthy options.
- You have a candy dish on your desk.
- The pantry is in close proximity to your home office.
- The break room at work is stocked with unhealthy, free snacks.
- Your child opens snacks and doesn't finish them, and rather than "waste" them, you finish them.

After you make your list, you might feel bad about yourself. That's normal. Don't let it overtake you. You have the courage to examine your behavior and make a change. That takes guts! (This is also why you'll want to wait to unwind bad habits until *after* you have positive momentum and success with creating new habits.)

With your contributing behaviors in hand, which do you tackle first?

Just like the exercise from the last chapter on how to choose behaviors that will help achieve a goal, choose to tackle the one on your list that's easiest and the one you want to do most. And if there are any one-time behaviors, do those first.

DESIGN BAD HABITS OUT OF YOUR LIFE, STARTING WITH THE TRIGGER

Now that you have your first targeted behaviors to stop, look to its trigger. We start with the trigger because it is usually the easiest to deal with. You can remove it (ideally), avoid it, or ignore it.

In the snacking example, what's the trigger? Is it the stocked pantry at home? If so, you're the master of your domain. You can remove the snacks from your home or relegate them to the back of the cabinet where you can't see them. This might be sufficient to end the habit.

Also of note, is removing the trigger something you need to do once, like ridding the pantry of snacks? Or is it a repeated action to remove it? Like putting your phone on Do Not Disturb every time you sit down to work to remove notification triggers, for example.

If you can't remove the trigger and need to avoid it, what does that look like? Is it abstaining from people, places, media, and situations that cue or prompt the behavior? When I was newly sober, certain environments made me want to drink—because I was accustomed to drinking in them. The same was true for people who'd been drinking buddies. You may want to continue that relationship or frequenting that environment. If that's the case, create boundaries and mentally rehearse how you'll abstain from the behavior you're trying to stop ... before you're in the situation.

When we can't or don't want to avoid the prompt, as in the example above, we're left with our last resort—ignoring it. This is dangerous territory because it has us relying on our fair-weather friends—willpower and motivation. Like we discussed in the last chapter, if this is your only option, mentally rehearse ignoring (or avoiding) the prompt and celebrate the moment you do—both in the mental rehearsal and in real life.

LOWER YOUR CAPABILITY

If removing, avoiding, or ignoring the trigger doesn't work, the next step is reducing your capability to do the habit—or making it harder to do.

Look to the R-cubed factors: the resources of time, money, knowledge and skills, tools, and assistance; rigor, whether it be physical, mental, or emotional; or the reach of your current routine. How can you weaken one or more of these factors?

Let's return to the unhealthy snacking example. WTF? (Where's the friction ... or lack thereof?) What is making it easy to snack? Consider the examples below and how they translate to the habits you want to unwind.

The pantry is stocked. It takes almost no time to grab a snack. But what if you removed all the unhealthy snacks from your house? The next time you got a hankering for chips, you'd have to get dressed, put on your shoes, and drive to the store. That takes time, money, and physical rigor, and that might be enough of a deterrent to keep you from going shopping.

There are free snacks in the breakroom at work. But what if they were placed in a vending machine and were no longer free? Depending on the cost, it might be enough to stop you. If you still find yourself buying Skittles, what if the prices were raised? What amount of money would make you say no? What if every time you bought Skittles, you had to put the same amount of money into a savings account? Or what if you had to donate the equivalent amount to the coffers of an organization completely opposed to your values? Note which of these feel the most off-putting ... that might be where you'll find gold.

What if you didn't remove the unhealthy snacks in your home, but instead stored them in a box in the attic or in the garage, high on a shelf that required you to get a ladder to reach it? I know you're not storing food in the garage or attic, but you get the idea. How can you make it physically harder to snack?

Inadvertently, we removed this capability factor and made snacking difficult in our last home. Our daughter had started to walk, and she was *constantly* going into the pantry, helping herself to snacks. Our pantry had a door, but she figured out how to open it and the child locks. We had to figure out how could we make it harder (or impossible) for her to open the door. The solution we came up with was to change the doorknob to one with a lock and key.

It worked like a charm, but here's what happened that we didn't expect: my husband also stopped snacking! He's in denial about it, but this guy seriously loves his snacks. (Sorry honey, this isn't libel because truth is a defense.) Even though the key to the lock was in a drawer only six feet away, the locked door caused enough friction (through physical rigor) to deter him. It also required presence of mind to get the key and unlock the door. I imagine his internal dialogue was something like, *Am I actually hungry, or am I thirsty, bored, a creature of habit, or all of the above?*

Just like making something physically easier to do is potent in creating new habits, making things physically harder to do is extremely effective in stopping them.

Putting a behavior out of reach from an existing routine its part of is the most difficult factor to adjust. For it to work, you would need to find a way for the existing habit to conflict with something you value or deem more important. Let's say you love a certain gym teacher's class. She begins to teach her class at a different, earlier time—5 a.m. You're in the habit of staying up late. You know you can't wake up in time to make it or have the energy required for a 5 a.m. class if you stay up late. You value going to her class more than staying up late, and so you go to bed earlier.

As discussed in Chapter 17, ambition is the last component of the behavior formula we tinker with. It's unreliable and, when it fails, we can equate this to being a failure ourselves. Hopefully, adjusting the trigger or capability factors help you stop your unwanted habit, but if not, you can reduce your ambition or desire to do something by manipulating satisfaction. You can make it less (or completely un-) satisfying. Or you can make the reward for *not* doing it more satisfying than the reward for doing the behavior.

Reflect on what makes you want to perform this unwanted behavior in the first place. Is it to fit in socially? Does it make you feel a certain way? Because you have a craving that's pulling you to the behavior?

Back to the snacking example. Now you know my husband loves to snack. If I said, "Hey honey, I'm going to try to stop snacking all month. Want to join me?" Or, "Hey sweetheart, I know you want to stop snacking, so for every day you don't snack this month, I'll reward you in the bedroom that night." (Actually, the latter is a great idea. Too bad we haven't been able to stop our daughter's habit of sleeping in our bed every night! Sort of like how the cobbler's children have no shoes. I digress, but you get the point.)

You can see how both of those invitations might lower his desire to snack by introducing a more enticing behavior in its place. Sex is more satisfying than snacking (hopefully), so this might work. (Especially if he celebrates not snacking and releases dopamine to associate snack abstinence with the neurochemical reward.) This example also layers in a social component. This is where accountability partners shine. (And no, sex doesn't need to be involved!) It seems like finding an accountability partner or group is often the first approach with habits, but unless the desire to uphold the agreement is stronger than the desire, capability, or trigger to do the behavior, accountability won't work. And you'll be left feeling bad about yourself when it doesn't.

Another way to reduce desire is to find something that will actively demotivate you. When I was trying to convert myself into a morning person at my first tech sales job, someone gave me this idea. I didn't do it because it scared the hell out of me, but it'll give you an idea of how demotivation works.

For that job, I needed to be in the office at 6 a.m. That meant a wake-up time of 4:30 a.m. I hadn't converted to an early riser yet, and to say I struggled making it into the office on time would be an understatement. Here's the terrible (although likely effective) idea a colleague gave to solve my problem. The night before, schedule an extremely humiliating social media post to go live at 4:35 a.m. If I wake up on time, I can prevent it from being posted. If not, utter embarrassment.

While I never tried this because I was too worried something would go wrong and it would post regardless of me waking up on time, I really detest this type of demotivation because it relies on shame. And shame is *not* how we create long-term change and transformation.

Here's another example of demotivating yourself. Going to a high-end dinner and playing "cell phone roulette." Essentially, you put your phones in a pile in the center of the table, and whoever reaches for their phone first pays for the entire tab. This relies on you being more motivated to not spend a few hundred bucks on dinner than you are to use your phone.

You can demotivate yourself by acquiring knowledge about the harmful effects of the behavior you want to stop. I know people who became vegans because of what they learned in the documentary *Forks Over Knives*.

A final example of demotivating yourself is to tap into a stronger motivation—like holding onto your money or reputation. What if every time you did the behavior you wanted to stop, you had to Venmo money to a friend who agreed to hold you accountable?

In each of these examples, notice how two of the behavior components—satisfaction and ambition—go hand in hand with designing our way out of a habit. Use them with caution and as a last resort. They are a slippery slope to shame and eroded confidence. Always start with capability and trigger.

IF ALL ELSE FAILS, DIAL IT BACK

When I quit drinking, I was primarily dealing with a behavioral and process addiction. I had wired in the behavior of cracking a beer or opening a bottle of wine as soon as work ended. And during the COVID pandemic's "shelter in place" protocols that never seemed to end, I was lucky to make it until 4 p.m.

I resisted quitting for a long time because of this behavioral— or process—addiction and the dopamine hit that followed. And I couldn't imagine life without it, socially and culturally. Thoughts like, *What will I do when I'm at dinner and there's a toast? How can I say no to drinking wine when I travel to France / Italy / Napa / South Africa?* If I wasn't so far out from my sobriety date and with the identity shift that's taken place, I'd still find these questions daunting.

Depending on how deeply ingrained the habit is that you're looking to stop, saying goodbye to it might feel like parting ways with a loved one or friend. We can get really attached to our behaviors and their associated emotions and identities.

If you find yourself struggling to quit something "forever," dial it back. You don't need to commit to that right now. Focus on today. Rinse and repeat. You've probably heard that "what fires together wires together," regarding brain synapses, and the reverse is also true. It takes as little as three weeks for neural pathways to begin weakening when they stop firing together through the same habitual thoughts, emotions, and actions.[84] Another adage that fits here: "Use it or lose it."

Think of this like the pruning necessary for a rose bush to thrive. You're mindfully pruning what's diverting energy from the beautiful buds that want to flourish.

SWAP IT

Swapping was an absolute lifeline for me on the journey to becoming alcohol-free. I don't think I would've been successful long-term if not for this strategy. Stocking the fridge with nonalcoholic beers and sparkling water was critical in the early days. Especially for *process* and *behavior* addictions. I was addicted to the process and behavior of opening the drink, holding the glass, and drinking from it to wind down—and, of course, the reward chemicals from the habit.

Leverage the behavior design skills you've learned from Chapters 17 and 18 to ideate behaviors that you can substitute for the habit you're looking to stop.

You can also remap the trigger. I did this without realizing that it's an actual behavior design strategy. The end of the workday was the prompt to drink alcohol. I remapped the prompt so that instead, the end of the workday meant it was time to open a nonalcoholic beer or sparkling water.

To swap in a new behavior, you'll want to remove (or minimize) the trigger of the unwanted behavior, and make it harder to do. In the example of going alcohol-free, maybe that means removing alcohol from your home, keeping it out of sight, or putting it somewhere inconvenient or that's hard to reach without a step stool.

If the swap isn't taking hold, don't distress. Perhaps it wasn't the right habit to replace the old one with. Go back to the list of ideas you created for the behavior swap and try another.

The great news is that you know all the fundamentals necessary to succeed with habits. You know how to troubleshoot. You know that tricky behaviors you can't stop or habits that won't stick are not personal flaws, but merely design flaws that need further troubleshooting.

IT'S GOING TO BE WORTH IT

If stopping habits was easy, everyone would do it. It's not, but I promise it'll be worth it. I can personally attest to this.

Imagine your life if you stop the habits keeping you from your full capacity and gifts. Think of the freed up spiritual, emotional, mental, and physical energy when rid of these behaviors! The world is your oyster. What experiences await you if you commit to doing this? If you commit to troubleshooting until you find what works? Who will be impacted by you making this commitment, continuing the mindset work, and taking the actions you're being called to?

It takes conscious awareness and continued recommitment to override our brain's wiring and the nonstop chatter of Pam and the ego. But what awaits you on the other side as your Higher Self? I'm still a work in progress, but I can attest to how the progress feels, and it is glorious.

Since I threw myself into this process in the summer of 2022, I have changed so much it's shocking. I am a far better wife, mother, friend, and daughter. I notice the little things in life that are the most precious and beautiful, that otherwise would've remained outside of my perception. I feel like I have a direct line to God. My connections with others are deeper and more meaningful. People tell me regularly that I've helped them quit drinking, do something that scared them, or take bold and courageous action. And I'm just getting started. *Who is waiting for your impact and message?*

Part Five: Ascend and Amplify

"Happiness is not a station you arrive at, but a manner of traveling."
—Norman MacEwen

Chapter 20

You Are Revolutionary

"The growth of understanding follows an ascending spiral rather than a straight line."

—Marion Milner

To do this work, and to become a better version of yourself is truly revolutionary. And you're *being* her and *doing* it. You're creating fundamental change, inside and out. And what's more, you've completed a revolution in the upward spiral that is your Higher Self ascension.

As this journey continues, refining our identity and habits as we grow and evolve will be necessary—and dare I say, liberating! You now have the mindset, knowledge, and resources to continually tap into your truth and design a life you love and are deeply fulfilled by.

Sometimes you might feel like you're going in circles, but maybe all you need is a perspective shift. When we're caught up in the daily minutiae, it's easy to feel like we're making little to no progress. But remember, tiny changes compound!

If you're "doing the work" and feel as though your progress is like this:

I invite you to shift your perspective. Look from another angle, and see it like this:

We're playing an infinite game, and I believe our unique upward spirals continue into eternity. That doesn't mean there won't be setbacks along the way. Without a doubt, there will be. And that's what makes us stronger. With every repetition of your aligned thoughts, words, and actions, you continue to strengthen these muscles and step further into the desired identity of your Higher Self.

By *being* and *doing* in the energy of your Higher Self, you will *have* her experience. Notably, you'll have what money can never buy: a vital physical body, a peaceful mind, and an abundantly loving soul.

As you continue the beautiful journey of your life and unlock new levels of growth and abundance, remember the five steps in the *Higher Self Habits* method for whatever comes your way:

1. **Aware:** What has come into your awareness and how do you perceive it?
2. **Align:** How would the best version of you—your Higher Self—think, be, and act in this situation?
3. **Audit:** What do you need to stop, start, or continue to realign with your Higher Self?
4. **Activate:** How can you take action as your Higher Self?
5. **Ascend and Amplify:** What's the next level you're raising your baseline to, and how can you make a greater impact in the world?

You've reached the final stage—ascension and amplification. Now the process begins again, with new levels of awareness, alignment, auditing, and activation. As you complete additional revolutions in your upward spiral, you'll amplify an energy that will magnetize your desires and be a healing force for good in your home, community, and in the world. Your Higher Self— this version of you—has been here within you all along. Now it's time for her to shine.

A FINAL BE HER NOW EXERCISE:

I invite you to renew your commitment.

> I, [your name] _____, commit
> to becoming my Higher Self!
> I commit to making myself a priority.
> I commit to bringing forth my gifts to the world.
> I commit to owning my identity as a divine child of
> God / the universe / a Higher Power.
> I commit to keeping an open mind and open heart.
> I commit to learning to fall in love with the
> process.
> I commit to having ears to hear and eyes to see
> as miracles begin unfolding all around me, and I
> intend to notice them.
> I commit to creating a positive ripple effect in the
> world, simply by being the best version of me.

Now, put your hand over your heart and say this aloud: "I commit to becoming my Higher Self!"

Then touch your head with your index finger and say: "I have everything within me to BE HER NOW!"

WHAT'S NEXT?

If you enjoyed this book and found it valuable, or if you are seeking continued support, I invite you to look at the programs I offer. There is truly something for everyone, in terms of both investment level and program length. Each offering explores the content of this book (and more!) in varying depths.

To learn more about ways we can work together, please visit alessiacitro.com/programs.

With love and gratitude, I wish you a beautiful, continued journey.

A Plea to Your Higher Self

Thank you for reading my book!

This book was written for you. I appreciate your feedback and want to hear it. In fact, I need your input to improve the next versions of this book. Your candid feedback will help shape my future books, too!

Here's the other reason I'm making this plea: reviews tremendously affect a book's success and how many others will find it. The more reviews (positive ones, especially) a book receives, the more Amazon's algorithm recommends it to other readers like you. If you got value from this book, would you be so kind as to pay it forward and leave a review?

Specifically, can you take two minutes right now to leave a review on Amazon?
alessiacitro.com/bookreview

Thank you so much!

—Alessia Citro

Appendix
Addiction Resources

If you or someone you know is struggling with addiction, remember that you're not alone. Seeking help is a courageous step toward reclaiming your life and well-being. I've been there, and I promise it gets better!

Below are some resources to assist you on your journey:

National Helpline: The Substance Abuse and Mental Health Services Administration offers a confidential, 24/7 helpline providing free referral for, and information on, treatment facilities, support groups, and other resources. Call 1-800-662-HELP (4357) or visit their website at www.samhsa.gov/find-help/national-helpline.

Alcoholics Anonymous (AA): A global fellowship of individuals who share their experiences, strength, and hope to help each other recover from alcoholism. Visit www.aa.org to find meetings near you or access online resources.

Narcotics Anonymous (NA): Like AA, NA provides support for individuals recovering from drug addiction. Find meetings and resources at www.na.org.

SMART Recovery: A science-based, self-empowering addiction recovery support group. Explore their online resources and find local meetings at www.smartrecovery.org.

Addiction Center: An online resource offering information on various types of addiction, treatment options, and support services. Visit www.addictioncenter.com for articles, helplines, and treatment directories.

Books: Consider reading books like *Clean: Overcoming Addiction and Ending America's Greatest Tragedy* by David Sheff, *Quit Like a Woman: The Radical Choice to Not Drink in a Culture Obsessed with Alcohol* by Holly Whitaker, or *The Recovering: Intoxication and Its Aftermath* by Leslie Jamison for personal insights and understanding.

Remember, recovery is a journey, and it's okay to reach out for help whenever you need it. You are worthy of support and healing.

RECOMMENDED READING

I'm a voracious reader and joke that I traded booze for books. The year I quit drinking, I read forty-eight books! Reading has grown me in immeasurable ways, and I want to share the most impactful books in my library with you. I've compiled a list of my favorite titles across the genres of spirituality, business, and personal development. Go to alessiacitro.com/book to download it.

Acknowledgments

This book would not have been possible without the help and support of many people. It takes a village to birth a book.

Laura Kaiser, thank you for the being you and the editor I prayed for. I knew from the moment I met you on Zoom that you were the one! Your belief in me, guidance, valuable input, and perspective took this book from a *rough* first draft to what it became—a work I am proud of. Truly, you helped me reclaim my voice and my authority. I will be forever grateful to you. Thank you.

Cheryl Isaac, thank you for your meticulous proofreading of this book. Your keen eye and thoughtful suggestions added the final touches and brought out the best in my work. Thank you for your invaluable contribution and for your kindness and encouragement.

Jake Kelfer, "thank you" isn't enough. Thank you for your immaculate follow-up game and for staying in touch with me for two years until I finally had *my* book. I could not have written this without the Big Idea to Bestseller program and community, and certainly not without your coaching and accountability. You pushed me far outside of my comfort zone, and I am better for it. Thank you for being such a supporter and cheerleader. I look forward to seeing what else I create with you in my corner.

Dr. Jenn Chrisman, thank you for being one of my greatest teachers and for writing the beautiful foreword of this book. Thank you for helping me continually soften, surrender, and explore the depths and peaks with gentle curiosity. Because of you, I am a better human, wife, mother, friend, daughter, and sister.

Lisa Boettcher, thank you for helping me lean boldly into my true essence with your vision and creative direction. I am so grateful to have met you, to call you a friend, and to have my brand modernized and elevated through your creative genius. (Shoutout to Sandy Critides for making that intro!)

Ginger Hamilton, thank you for seeing my vision for the cover and running with it. Your handwriting was the magic the cover needed to become what I saw in my mind's eye. I am incredibly thankful that fate sat us together at Lisa Boettcher's dinner party. Cheers to all the collaboration to come!

James Clear and Dr. BJ Fogg, thank you for making habits accessible to the masses and a topic of needed conversation. Your books were the lever that opened the door to me changing my own habits—and thus my life. You demystified the topic and ignited my curiosity through your powerful works. (If you enjoyed this book, read theirs if you haven't yet! Both *Atomic Habits* and *Tiny Habits* can be found in the recommended reading list at alessiacitro.com/book.)

Dr. Joe Dispenza, thank you for literally opening my mind. Your books have been a key catalyst in my personal growth journey—particularly for awakening me to the power of the quantum field and my own mind. Thank you for blazing a trail and sharing your field guide in an accessible way the world can benefit from.

For my Instagram community, thank you for your support along this arduous journey! Without you, your votes on polls, and your kind and candid feedback, this book would quite literally look different. And, it would not have been nearly as much fun to create *Higher Self Habits* without you at the forefront of my mind as I wrote. Thank you for inspiring and encouraging me every step of the way. The victory of finishing this project is shared with each of you!

Jenny Burnham, thank you for being one of my biggest supporters and for being a living testament to the power of the method within this book. You were this book's first *reader*, and I will be forever grateful for your valuable feedback and encouragement. If everyone had a friend and supporter like you in their corner, there is nothing that could not be accomplished.

Alessandra Sollevare, Brie Johnson, Harley Jordan, Holly Stein, Liz Garcia, and Mel Tingey. Thank you for being my entrepreneurial running buddies. I could not have written this book without your unwavering support. Thank you for always being willing to give feedback, shoot me straight, and cheer me on. You were the first to buy preorder copies of this book. Knowing you had my back throughout the process was instrumental in crossing the finish line. Thank you to the moon and back.

Jackie Erin, Jackie Kurtz, Kristen Tener, Liz Ward, Sandy Critides, and Shannon van Heerden. Thank you for being supportive and loving friends throughout the writing journey. Your presence in my life and ride-or-die friendships helped steady me throughout a tumultuous process—whether you knew it or not. No matter if this book bombs or sells millions of copies, I've known all along that you girls will be there for me and will remain my friends. There's no stating how much that means and how much I love y'all.

Dad, thank you for being my entrepreneurial inspiration and the walking testament to what is possible through vision, belief, and the action to make it happen. Some of my favorite traits I inherited from you are my drive, dreaming, and work ethic. You and I just won't quit, and I'm so grateful to have learned that from you. Thank you for always having my back and for bringing out my potential, even from a young age. I love you.

Mom, I could write a book acknowledging you alone. Honestly, I couldn't have done this without you. There are the tangible reasons, like watching your beautiful granddaughter at times so I could write ... or take a needed break from writing. Then there are the many intangibles. Your love and encouragement are second to none. This book could be widely repurposed as a doorstop, and I know you'd love me anyway. There's no way to convey just how much that knowledge helped me bring this to life. Thank you for being you and for being the most incredible mother walking the earth. Your loving presence, eternal calm, and cheerful disposition inspire me every day. People complain that they become their mother as they age, but with you, it would be an honor. I hope to emulate you more and more as the days go by. No wonder my soul chose you. I love you.

Jeff, there is too much to say. I knew full well that I was marrying an incredible man, but nearly a decade later, you continue to surprise and delight with the depths of your love and support. At time of publication, it will have been three years exactly since the fateful day I knew I had to leave the corporate world. In that time, I have made many wrong turns and paid a great deal of tuition to the school of life. You've loved and stood by me through it all. You have supported me in *every way* a partner can. To say I'm grateful doesn't scratch the surface. Thank you to the ends of the universe for choosing me every day and for believing in me as I brought this vision to life. And thank you for the many late nights and weekends you did solo dad duty so I could finish this book. If it wasn't for you, it would not exist. I love you for eternity.

My Mila, thank you for being the fuel and guiding light as I continue my journey of ascension into the best version of me. I pursue my Higher Self because of *you*, my darling girl. For as long as I live, I will never forget the night, shortly before publication, when the manuscript was done and I was filled with doubt, crying. You calmly came to check on me and with a palpable certainty, you said, "I believe in you, Mama." You are such a wise, kind, and loving soul, and I am next-level blessed to be your mom. Thank you for being unapologetically you and for healing me in ways I didn't know were possible. I look forward to a lifetime of making ripples and waves with you.

Endnotes

1. "Stewardship," Merriam-Webster.com Dictionary, accessed January 30, 2024, https://www.merriam-webster.com/dictionary/stewardship.

2. Rollin McCraty, Mike Atkinson, and Dana Tomasino. "Modulation of DNA Conformation by Heart-Focused Intention." HeartMath Institute, 2003.

3. "Faith," Merriam-Webster.com Dictionary, accessed January 30, 2024, https://www.merriam-webster.com/dictionary/faith.

4. Formula for calculation is $A=P(1+r)n$. A is the amount of improvement at the end of year. P is the initial value (1, in this case). r is the rate of improvement, or daily interest rate of 0.5 percent, which is 0.005 as a decimal. n is the number of days for compounding, which is 365.

5. Lee, Hau L., and Billington, Corey. "The Evolution of Supply-Chain-Management Models and Practice at Hewlett-Packard." *Interfaces* 25, no. 5 (1995): 42-63.

6. Abigail Player, Georgina Randsley de Moura, Ana C. Leite, Fatima Tresh, and Dominic Abrams. "Overlooked Leadership Potential: The Preference for Leadership Potential in Job Candidates Who Are Men vs. Women." *Frontiers in Psychology* 10 (2019): 755. https://doi.org/10.3389/fpsyg.2019.00755.

7. Women's Business Ownership Act of 1988, Pub. L. No. 100-533, 102 Stat. 2689 (1988).

8. O'Connor v. Donaldson, 422 U.S. 563 (1975).

9. "First Self-Made Millionairess," Guinness World Records. Accessed March 17, 2024. https://www.guinnessworldrecords.com/world-records/first-self-made-millionairess.

10. "Madam C.J. Walker - Biography, Entrepreneur, Inventor." Biography.com. Accessed March 17, 2024. https://www.biography.com/business-leaders/madam-cj-walker.

11. Brendon Burchard, High Performance Habits: How Extraordinary People Become That Way (Carlsbad, CA: Hay House, Inc., 2017)

12. Stephen R. Covey, *The 7 Habits of Highly Effective People: Powerful Lessons in Personal Change* (New York: Simon & Schuster, 1989)

13. Stephen R. Covey, *The 7 Habits of Highly Effective People: Powerful Lessons in Personal Change* (New York: Simon & Schuster, 1989)

14. Mark F. Bear, Barry W. Connors, and Michael A. Paradiso. *Neuroscience: Exploring the Brain*. 4th ed. (Philadelphia: Wolters Kluwer, 2016)

15. Jaak Panksepp, "Affective Neuroscience of the Emotional Brainmind: Evolutionary Perspectives And Implications For Understanding Depression." *Dialogues in Clinical Neuroscience* 12, no. 4 (2010): 533-545.

16. Georg Northoff, and Jaak Panksepp. "The trans-species concept of self and the subcortical–cortical midline system." *Trends in Cognitive Sciences* 12, no. 7 (2008): 259-264.

17. Richard E. Passingham, and Steven P. Wise. *The Neurobiology of the Prefrontal Cortex: Anatomy, Evolution, and the Origin of Insight*. Oxford: Oxford University Press, 2012.

18. Bélanger, Mireille, Igor Allaman, and Pierre J. Magistretti. "Brain Energy Metabolism: Focus on Astrocyte-Neuron Metabolic Cooperation." *Cell Metabolism* 14, no. 6 (December 7, 2011): 724-738. doi:10.1016/j.cmet.2011.08.016.

19. J.B. Taylor, *My Stroke of Insight: A Brain Scientist's Personal Journey*. (New York: Viking, 2008)

20. Pauline R. Clance and Suzanne A. Imes. "The Impostor Phenomenon in High Achieving Women: Dynamics and Therapeutic Intervention." Psychotherapy: Theory, Research & Practice, vol. 15, no. 3, 1978, pp. 241-247.

21. Lucas S. LaFreniere, Michelle G. Newman, "Exposing Worry's Deceit: Percentage of Untrue Worries" in Generalized Anxiety Disorder Treatment, Behavior Therapy, Volume 51, Issue 3, 2020, Pages 413-423, ISSN 0005-7894, https://doi.org/10.1016/j.beth.2019.07.003. (https://www.sciencedirect.com/science/article/pii/S0005789419300826)

22. Robert L. Leahy, *The Worry Cure: Seven Steps to Stop Worry from Stopping You* (New York: Harmony Books, 2005)

23. "Fine-tuned Universe." Encyclopedia MDPI. Last modified 2021. https://encyclopedia.pub/entry/27760.

24. Robert Lanza, and Bob Berman. *Biocentrism: How Life and Consciousness Are the Keys to Understanding the True Nature of the Universe*. (Dallas, TX: BenBella Books, Inc., 2009)

25. Stephen R. Covey, *The 7 Habits of Highly Effective People: Powerful Lessons in Personal Change*. (New York: Free Press, 1989)

26. W. E. Hill, "My wife and my mother-in-law. They are both in this picture - find them." Photomechanical print, November 6, 1915. Created by William Ely Hill.

27. Joe Dispenza, *Evolve Your Brain: The Science of Changing Your Mind*. Health Communications, Inc., 2007.

28. Elizabeth A. Phelps, et al. "Emotion and Cognition: Insights from Studies of the Human Amygdala." *Annual Review of Psychology*, vol. 57, 2006, pp. 27–53.

29. Daniel David, et al. "Why Cognitive Behavioral Therapy Is the Current Gold Standard of Psychotherapy." *Frontiers in Psychiatry*, vol. 9, 2018, Article 4.

30. Robert K. Merton, "The Self-fulfilling Prophecy." *Antioch Review*, vol. 8, no. 2, 1948, pp. 193–210.

31. Lipton H. Bruce *The Biology of Belief: Unleashing the Power of Consciousness, Matter & Miracles*. (New York: Hay House, Inc., 2008)

32. Fabrizio Benedetti, et al. "Placebo and the New Physiology of the Doctor-Patient Relationship." *Physiological Reviews*, vol. 93, no. 3, 2013, pp. 1207–1246.

33. Ted J. Kaptchuk, Elizabeth Friedlander, John M. Kelley, M. Norma Sanchez, Efi Kokkotou, Joyce P. Singer, Magda Kowalczykowski, et al. "Placebos without Deception: A Randomized Controlled Trial in Irritable Bowel Syndrome." PLoS ONE 5, no. 12 (December 22, 2010): e15591. doi:10.1371/journal.pone.0015591.

34. Amit Goswami, *The Self-Aware Universe: How Consciousness Creates the Material World*. TarcherPerigee, 1995.

35. Lynne McTaggart, *The Field: The Quest for the Secret Force of the Universe*. (New York: Harper Perennial, 2008)

36. Eckhart Tolle, *The Power of Now: A Guide to Spiritual Enlightenment*. (Novato, CA: New World Library, 1999)

37. Wayne W. Dyer, *Wishes Fulfilled: Mastering the Art of Manifesting*. (New York: Hay House, Inc., 2012)

38. Kent C. Berridge and Terry E. Robinson. "What is the Role of Dopamine in Reward: Hedonic Impact, Reward Learning, or Incentive Salience?" Brain Research Reviews 28, no. 3 (1998): 309-369.

39. Jacobo Grinberg-Zylberbaum, M. Delaflor, M. E. Sanchez Arellano, Guevara, and M. Pérez. "Human Communication and the Electrophysiological Activity of the Brain." Subtle Energies & Energy Medicine Journal Archives 3 (1992). https://api.semanticscholar.org/CorpusID:59169981.

40. John S., Hagelin, David W. Orme-Johnson, Maxwell V. Rainforth, Kenneth L. Cavanaugh, Charles N. Alexander, Susan F. Shatkin, John L. Davies, Anne O. Hughes, and Emanuel Ross. "Effects of Group Practice of the Transcendental Meditation Program on Preventing Violent Crime in Washington, D.C.: Results of the National Demonstration Project, June–July 1993." Social Indicators Research 47, no. 2 (December 1999): 153–201.

41. Joe Dispenza, Breaking the Habit of Being Yourself: How to Lose Your Mind and Create a New One. (Carlsbad, CA: New York: Hay House, Inc., 2012)

42. Leonard Leibovici, "Effects of Remote, Retroactive Intercessory Prayer on Patients with Bloodstream Infections: Randomised Controlled Trial." BMJ 323 (2001): 1450-1451. https://doi.org/10.1136/bmj.323.7327.1450

43. BJ Fogg, Tiny Habits: The Small Changes That Change Everything. (Boston: Houghton Mifflin Harcourt, 2019)

44. F. R. Van der Weel, Ruud, and Audrey L. H. Van der Meer. "Handwriting but not typewriting leads to widespread brain connectivity: a high-density EEG study with implications for the classroom." Frontiers in Psychology (2024). https://doi.org/10.3389/fpsyg.2023.1219945

45. James W. Pennebaker, "Writing About Emotional Experiences as a Therapeutic Process." Psychological Science 8, no. 3 (1997): 162-166. https://doi.org/10.1111/j.1467-9280.1997.tb00403.x.

46. E. Niedermeyer and F. L da Silva, Electroencephalography: Basic Principles, Clinical Applications, and Related Fields. (Lippincott Williams & Wilkins, 2005)

47. Nadine Dijkstra et al. "Humans Struggle to Differentiate Imagination from Reality" UCL News, University College London, Apr. 2023, www.ucl.ac.uk/news/2023/apr/humans-struggle-differentiate-imagination-reality.

48. Tian-Ming Yen, "Culm Height Development, Biomass Accumulation and Carbon Storage in an Initial Growth Stage for a Fast-Growing Moso Bamboo (Phyllostachys Pubescens)." Botanical Studies 57, no. 10 (2016). https://doi.org/10.1186/s40529-016-0126-x.

49. David R. Hawkins,. *Power vs. Force: The Hidden Determinants of Human Behavior*. (Carlsbad, CA: Hay House, Inc., 2012)

50. Joe Dispenza,. *Becoming Supernatural: How Common People Are Doing the Uncommon*. (Carlsbad, CA: Hay House, Inc., 2017)

51. Raymond Faulkner and Ogden Goelet, eds. *The Egyptian Book of the Dead: The Book of Going Forth by Day. The Complete Papyrus of Ani Featuring Integrated Text and Full-Color Images*. (San Francisco: Chronicle Books, 1994)

52. Holy Bible, New International Version. *Proverbs* 4:23. (Grand Rapids: Zondervan, 2011)

53. Lini Wijngaards, "The Blackfoot Wisdom That Inspired Maslow's Hierarchy." *Resilience*, June 18, 2021. https://www.resilience.org/stories/2021-06-18/the-blackfoot-wisdom-that-inspired-maslows-hierarchy/.

54. NeuroGym Team. "New Study: You Have 6,200 Thoughts a Day ... Don't Make Yours Negative." NeuroGym, blog.myneurogym.com. Accessed March 31, 2024. (https://blog.myneurogym.com/new-study-you-have-6900-thoughts-a-day-dont-make-yours-negative/)

55. Lera Boroditsky, "Does Language Shape Thought? Mandarin and English Speakers' Conceptions of Time." Cognitive Psychology 43, no. 1 (2001): 1-22.

56. Orly Fuhrman, Kelly McCormick, Eva Chen, Heidi Jiang, Dingfang Shu, and Shuaimei Mao. "How Linguistic and Cultural Forces Shape Conceptions of Time: English and Mandarin Time in 3D." *Cognitive Science* 35, no. 7 (2011): 1305-1328. https://doi.org/10.1111/j.1551-6709.2011.01193.x.

57. Jonathan Winawer, Nathan Witthoft, Michael C. Frank, Lisa Wu, Alex R. Wade, and Lera Boroditsky. "Russian Blues Reveal Effects of Language on Color Discrimination." Proceedings of the National Academy of Sciences 104, no. 19 (2007): 7780-7785.

58. Anna Wierzbicka, *Emotions across Languages and Cultures: Diversity and Universals* (Cambridge: Cambridge University Press, 1999)

59. Zoltán Kövecses, *Metaphor and Emotion: Language, Culture, and Body in Human Feeling* (Cambridge: Cambridge University Press, 2000)

60. Alia J. Crum and Ellen J. Langer. "Mind-Set Matters: Exercise and the Placebo Effect." *Psychological Science* 18, no. 2 (2007): 165-171. http://dx.doi.org/10.1111/j.1467-9280.2007.01867.x.

61. Ilan Dar-Nimrod and Steven J. Heine. "Exposure to Scientific Theories Affects Women's Math Performance." *Science* 314, no. 5798 (2006): 435. doi:10.1126/science.1131100.

62. Martin E.P. Seligman, *Learned Optimism: How to Change Your Mind and Your Life* (New York: Pocket Books, 1990)

63. Masaru Emoto, *The Hidden Messages in Water* (Hillsboro, OR: Beyond Words Publishing, 2004.)

64. U.S. Geological Survey. "The Water in You: Water and the Human Body." Accessed March 31, 2024. https://www.usgs.gov/special-topics/water-science-school/science/water-you-water-and-human-body.

65. Adam Hajo and Adam D. Galinsky. "Enclothed Cognition." Journal of Experimental Social Psychology 48, no. 4 (2012): 918-925.

66. Danielle King, @daniellekingstyle, direct communication via Instagram, January 14, 2024.

67. United Nations. "The Global Housing Crisis—Adequate Housing as a Component of the Right to an Adequate Standard of Living." United Nations Human Rights Office of the High Commissioner, 2020.

68. World Health Organization (WHO) and UNICEF. "Progress on Household Drinking Water, Sanitation, and Hygiene 2000-2020: Five Years into the SDGs." WHO/UNICEF Joint Monitoring Programme for Water Supply, Sanitation, and Hygiene (JMP), 2021.

69. Literacy, Inc., Accessed March 1, 2024, https://literacyinc.com/about.

70. Simon Kemp, "Digital 2023: Global Overview Report." DataReportal, 2023.

71. Natascha De Hoog and Peter Verboon. "Is the news making us unhappy? The influence of daily news exposure on emotional states." *British Journal of Psychology* 111, no. 157 (2020): 157-173. https://doi.org/10.1111/bjop.12389.

72. Shawn Achor and Michelle Gielan. "Consuming Negative News Can Make You Less Effective at Work." *Harvard Business Review.* September 2015. https://hbr.org/2015/09/consuming-negative-news-can-make-you-less-effective-at-work.

73. Bloomberg. "Here's How Quickly People Ditch Weight Loss Resolutions." Bloomberg.com. Last modified January 16, 2019. https://www.bloomberg.com/news/articles/2019-01-16/here-s-how-quickly-people-ditch-weight-loss-resolutions

74. Chapman, Gary. The 5 Love Languages: The Secret to Love that Lasts. (Chicago: Northfield Publishing, 2015.)

75. BJ Fogg, *Tiny Habits: The Small Changes That Change Everything* (Boston: Houghton Mifflin Harcourt, 2019)

76. "Why Most New Year's Resolutions Fail." *Lead Read Today* Fisher College of Business at The Ohio State University, February 2, 2023. Accessed March 3, 2024. https://fisher.osu.edu/blogs/leadreadtoday/why-most-new-years-resolutions-fail.

77. Richard M. Ryan and Edward L. Deci. *Self-Determination Theory: Basic Psychological Needs in Motivation, Development, and Wellness* (New York: Guilford Press, 2017)

78. Richard S., Sutton and Andrew G. Barto. *Reinforcement Learning: An Introduction Second Edition* (Cambridge, Massachusetts: The MIT Press, 2018)

79. James O. Prochaska, and Carlo C. DiClemente. *The Transtheoretical Approach: Crossing Traditional Boundaries of Therapy* (Malabar, FL: Krieger Publishing Company, 1984)

80. BJ Fogg, *Tiny Habits: The Small Changes That Change Everything* (Boston: Houghton Mifflin Harcourt, 2019)

81. James Clear, *Atomic Habits: An Easy & Proven Way to Build Good Habits & Break Bad Ones* (New York: Avery, 2018)

82. Kevin Dolak, "Teen Daughters Lift 3,000-Pound Tractor Off Dad." ABC *News*, April 1, 2013. https://abcnews.go.com/blogs/headlines/2013/04/teen-daughters-lift-3000-pound-tractor-off-dad.

83. Barry Michels and Phil Stutz. *Coming Alive: 4 Tools to Defeat Your Inner Enemy, Ignite Creative Expression & Unleash Your Soul's Potential* (New York: Spiegel & Grau, 2017)

84. Eric R. Kandel, James H. Schwartz, Thomas M. Jessell, Steven A. Siegelbaum, and A. J. Hudspeth. *Principles of Neural Science* 5th ed. (New York: McGraw-Hill, 2012.)

Printed in Great Britain
by Amazon

45054708R00179